"Ar ... ."

He o ... ue
eyes q ... iel
would

I'm sorry, Lord, I didn't mean to be sarcastic or disrespectful. The wisp of a prayer surprised him.

"I'm sorry, Savannah. Gabriel has tried to teach me about God and His love for us. Sometimes I do stupid things without thinking." Shane relaxed his arms on his legs, palms up in a partial shrug. "That right there was a perfect example. If a person is going to talk to God, he should do it with respect and reverence."

Gabriel picked that moment to walk up.

"Shane, there's something I need to tell you—" He perused Shane's upturned arms. "What are you doing?"

"I was waiting for God to drop a ma for Vannah on my lap."

"I see." Gabriel shook his head, used to Shane's oddities. "As I was saying—"

A shrill scream filled the air, and a bedraggled woman fell from above, landing perfectly in Shane's relaxed arms.

PAIGE WINSHIP DOOLY is the author of over a dozen books and novellas. She enjoys living in the coastal Deep South with her family, after having grown up in the sometimes extremely cold Midwest. She is happily married to her high school sweetheart and loves their life of adventure in a full house with six homeschooled children, a cat, and three dogs.

Books by Paige Winship Dooly

HEARTSONG PRESENTS
HP84—Heart's Desire
HP775—Treasure in the Hills
HP807—The Greatest Find
HP820—Carousel Dreams
HP840—The Petticoat Doctor
HP903—The Lightkeeper's Daughter

The Displaced Belle

Paige Winship Dooly

Heartsong Presents

For our newest "Belle," Ashton Mackenzie!
We love you so much!

A note from the Author:
I love to hear from my readers! You may correspond with me by writing:

Paige Winship Dooly
Author Relations
PO Box 721
Uhrichsville, OH 44683

ISBN 978-1-60260-993-8

THE DISPLACED BELLE

All scripture quotations are taken from the King James Version of the Bible.

All of the characters and events in this book are fictitious. Any resemblance to actual persons, living or dead, or to actual events is purely coincidental.

Our mission is to publish and distribute inspirational products offering exceptional value and biblical encouragement to the masses.

PRINTED IN THE U.S.A.

one

Outskirts of Atlanta, Georgia, 1870

"You aren't going in the saloon, Shane." Gabriel clutched his ever-present Bible and held it tight against his chest. The sun's slanted rays shone against the black leather of the worn book. "We have things to do."

Shane wanted to grab the Good Book, thump it upside Gabriel's tilted head, and remove his friend's smug expression.

Instead of acting on the tempting—but inappropriate—thought, Shane raised an eyebrow and glared at his annoyingly self-righteous friend. "I'm not going to the saloon, you say?" He settled back against the plank wall of the storefront, crossed his arms, and glared. The aroma of fried chicken from the kitchen of the boarding house two doors behind him wafted by and momentarily distracted him, setting his mouth to watering. He struggled to keep his focus on Gabriel while his stomach rumbled in protest.

Gabriel's eyes widened as he stared Shane down, the whites a stark contrast to his dark features. He shifted his stance and held his ground. "No. You're not going to the saloon. You have two little girls waiting for you, Shane. We need to get home to them."

"Those little girls probably don't even know I'm coming. One more night won't hurt them. And it's not like we can go without grabbing a bite to eat." He pushed off from the wall of the general store with a grin, problem solved. "We'll head out first thing in the morning and fetch 'em."

"Smelling of liquor and smoke," Gabriel muttered. He stepped between Shane and the saloon, effectively blocking his path. "Those sweet little girls don't need their older brother coming home reeking of cheap perfume."

"I'm going in to play a few hands of cards, Gabriel. Nothing more." Shane tightened his hands into fists and released them. He shifted to the left. If he moved fast, he could duck around Gabriel and be halfway down the walkway before Gabriel knew what happened. One thing Gabriel hated was making a scene. This little interlude had to be unnerving his friend as it was.

Gabriel watched and countered, his eyes narrowing. He straightened the fingers of his free hand and wiggled them, a telltale sign of his frustration. His eyes were alert for Shane's next move.

Shane stepped back to the right. All he wanted was an evening in the saloon. Just one, before he fetched the girls. He needed to feel the papery texture of the cards in his hands. He needed to smell the reassuring aromas of the saloon. He wouldn't imbibe, but he'd think about it. Imagine it. Dream about it. The saloon was his refuge, Gabriel his ubiquitous thorn in the flesh.

When Shane had befriended the skinny little misfit outside the schoolhouse twenty years earlier, he'd had no idea the frail boy would make it his life's purpose to "protect" Shane from himself.

Back then Gabriel had been the one who'd needed protecting. As a boy, Gabe would sneak up to the schoolhouse door and listen in on the lessons—something Shane found intriguing. Shane did everything he could to get kicked *out* of the schoolroom.

Gabriel's determination impressed Shane in some way, and he'd secured Gabriel a slate. He defended Gabriel when the other kids caught him listening in and taunted him.

Shane shook off the memories. Those were hard days for both of them. "No women, no liquor, just cards, Gabe. Is that so much to ask? After we get the girls, I won't have a chance to do anything like this until I find them another place to live." His voice trailed off. The girls were a handful. Placing them with a new family wouldn't be an easy task. "And we both know finding them another home could take a while."

"They've been with everyone we know, Shane. You're out of options. The girls wouldn't be nearly as challenging if you would take responsibility and raise them yourself as you should. They need their big brother. They want to be with you."

"I love the way you go from 'we' to 'you' when it comes to my options with the girls."

"Like I said, they need you." Gabriel shrugged and turned away, his attitude saying he'd won and there was no suitable response to his final comment.

"Oh come on, Gabe. You've been trying that whole back-to-the-world stance since we were boys. You should know by now it doesn't work on me."

"Nothing works on you, Shane," Gabe tossed over his shoulder. "You're unchangeable. I don't even know why I put up with you. You can't keep living your life this way."

Shane's laugh drew the attention of a group of women who also stood in front of the general store, the side nearer the saloon. One woman, a pretty blond, appraised him for a long moment. She turned back to her friends, but not before he'd sent her his charming trademark grin.

"Did you hear me?" Gabriel's voice interrupted the moment. "I'm talking to you, Shane."

"The question is, Gabriel, did you see her? She's breathtaking." Shane lounged back against the wall and watched her as she spoke to the other women.

"Your breath hasn't been taken. You're still talking to me." Gabriel remained where he was, facing the women's direction while keeping his back to Shane.

"Don't be so literal. Look at her." Arms folded, Shane tipped his head back against the wall, trying to see past Gabriel's silhouette. "She's different from the other women around here."

"You haven't been around 'here' for a while. How would you know what the women are like? You discerned that from her dismissive glance? You haven't even met her, Shane."

"So you did get a look at her. Her glance wasn't dismissive. She was flirting with me. Did you see her little smile?"

"No, but I did see her little boy. Or did you miss him? The little lad standing beside her and pulling at her skirts? Did you happen to notice *him*, Shane?"

"A child?" Shane shuddered and hurried to stand upright, peering at the child from over Gabriel's shoulder. "Well, that's that, then. We'd best be moving on."

"To get your sisters?"

"No. To get to the saloon."

Shane had tired of their sparring. He pushed past Gabriel just as the swinging doors of the saloon burst open. The wooden doors slammed back against the rough plank wall of the building as two men tumbled through. Patrons poured out from the saloon, yelling and inciting the fighting men.

The three women outside the general store screamed at the ruckus and scattered as the belligerent men punched and stumbled their way.

Shane moved through the chaos, grasped the larger man by

the collar, and yanked him out of the brawl. As drunk as the man was, he was no match for Shane's agile moves. Shane settled him on a nearby bench while the smaller man stepped back and wiped at his bloody lip.

"Thank you, sir. I owe you one."

"You don't owe me anything. If that ring on your finger is any indication, you owe someone else your presence. You have better places to be. Just get on home to your family and stay away from here." Shane caught the blond woman's eye and smiled. "The saloon isn't the place for a family man."

He heard Gabriel's judgmental intake of breath from slightly behind him. He ignored the insinuation. Shane wasn't a family man and planned to keep it that way.

"Oh my, did you *see* him, Lydia?" one of the older two women gushed from a few feet away. "That handsome man just stepped right in and ended the skirmish without as much as a thought for his own safety or well-being."

"Indeed, Lydie, have you ever seen such a brave, brave man?" a second voice joined in. "And to send that other man home to his family. Precious. You don't come across men like him very often these days."

Gabriel snorted.

Shane glanced over his shoulder. Judging by the location of the blond, she hadn't been one to speak. Instead she stood slightly to the side, surveying him through guarded eyes. This time he didn't miss the presence of the small boy who clung to her skirts in fear.

Shane tipped his hat at the trio and turned back to the drunk in front of him. "Let's get you inside and see if we can sober you up before you head home."

"Oh. Just a *perfect* gentleman," the first woman crooned. She tsked her tongue. "I need to marry a man like him."

The older women exchanged amused glances. They were having a great time at Shane's expense.

Marriage. Not a concept Shane wanted to think about. He preferred to move through life alone. It was bad enough Gabriel had attached himself to Shane's side, but after tomorrow he'd temporarily be saddled with his two little sisters as well.

"Help me out here, Gabe. This man has drawn enough attention for the day." Shane couldn't resist one more glance over his shoulder at the blond. Her green eyes widened as their gazes met, and without thinking he grinned at her and winked.

He'd *winked.* His spontaneous reaction startled him. He rubbed at his eye like he had a tic. He'd never winked at a proper woman—let alone one that was hitched—in all his life. Especially one with a watchful lad by her side. He saved that sort of nonsense for the nameless girls in the saloons. He was losing his touch. He turned and snatched the man off the bench with a bit more force than he'd meant to use and hauled him through the saloon doors.

❧

"Did you *see* that, Mavis? That darling man winked at our Lydia here."

"I don't think anyone with eyes missed that wink, Beatrice," Mavis tittered. "I thought my heart was going to melt right then and there. It was beautiful. Absolutely beautiful. And he couldn't take his eyes off her."

"Oh, I don't think he winked," Lydia corrected. Judging by the warmth in her cheeks, her face had to be red with embarrassment. "He merely had something in his eye. Didn't you see him rub it after? I'm sure it meant nothing. Poor fellow had his hands full with that inebriated man."

And Lydia had no tolerance for inebriated men. Her stepfather was one drunk too many as far as she was concerned. And speaking of. . .they needed to get going before he took issue with the length of time they'd been gone. "Come along, Wyatt. We need to finish our shopping and get home."

Wyatt resisted. "Aw, Lydie! I wanna watch the men fight some more. It just got interesting out here."

Lydia dropped to his level. "Wyatt. Men like that aren't interesting. They're pathetic. I wish you hadn't seen that interlude, and I want you to forget about it."

"Do I have to forget about the man who broke up the fight? Did you see him, Lydie? He just grabbed up that big, fat man and put him on that bench like it was nothin'."

"Nothing," Lydia corrected.

"I know! He was brave, Lydia. And he winked at you. I wanna learn to wink like that." Wyatt's face contorted, and his nose wrinkled as he squished both eyes tightly shut. "Did I wink at you like he did?"

Mavis and Beatrice laughed.

Lydia's face burned. "That's enough, Wyatt. He didn't wink at me. I told you. . .he had something in his eye."

Had he winked? Against her will, her heart beat a little faster at the thought. He was most definitely handsome, and she couldn't deny—to herself at least—that she enjoyed his attentions. She shook off her silly musings. Her stepfather's actions during the past decade had taught her that just because a man looked nice, didn't mean he was.

"I sure wish I coulda grabbed that fat man and put him on the bench like that. Bam! Sit there, you bad guy!"

Mavis and Beatrice's laughter abruptly stopped as they gasped at the vehemence in Wyatt's voice. Mavis's hand moved to her heart, and Beatrice fanned her face.

"Wyatt!" Lydia sent the two women an apologetic smile. "Children do say the silliest things, don't they?"

She turned to the small boy. "We mustn't talk like that about other people, Wy. You need to speak with respect, even if someone isn't making the best choice. And I don't want you to ever go near a man like that. It isn't proper. Promise me?"

Wyatt looked confused. "Then how can we go home to Daddy?"

Lydia closed her eyes. Her precocious brother was too perceptive for both of their own good. "It's different with Daddy. We'll talk about it on the way home. Right now, though, we need to go and gather up our supplies."

Wyatt shrugged, already moving on. "Do I still get my peppermint stick?"

"I don't know." Lydia laughed. "Are you *still* going to behave?"

"I always do, don't I?" He grinned.

They both knew that wasn't true. Wyatt could find more mischief than time to fit it all in.

Lydia couldn't help but notice that his grin contained all of the charm the flirtatious man at the saloon had exuded and then some—the man who most surely did wink at her. And here was Wyatt, bent on mimicking the man. Lydia could think of worse men for Wyatt to imitate, his own father topping the list. Still, she planned to raise Wyatt to be a steadfast, hardworking, and trustworthy man, not a flirt who tried to turn a woman's head. And to flirt with a woman who had a child hanging on her skirts at that! Surely such a thing would make most men think twice about her availability.

Lord, I'm going to need everything You've put in my arsenal when it comes to raising this one! Please help me prevent Wyatt from growing up to become anything like the charmer who walked into the saloon next door.

Lydia glanced down at her younger brother and sighed. He grinned up at her. With his golden ringlets and guileless blue eyes, she didn't stand a chance. He was a natural-born charmer.

❧

"You've brought yourself to a new low, Shane," Gabriel started in the minute they cleared the saloon's door. "You've deceived a lot of people in your life, but to act like you were only coming in here to sober that man up. . ." He clucked his tongue. "It's just wrong, Shane."

"I tried to get him to take the coffee. He wasn't interested." Shane glanced at the man who had pushed Shane away and had then collapsed just inside the saloon's doorway. He now lay curled on his side, snoring peacefully. "He looks content enough to me."

"That's not the point, and you know it. And you sent that other man home to his wife, then turned right around and got all flirty with that married woman on the walkway."

"I didn't flirt."

"You winked at her."

"I had something in my eye."

"I'm sure you did. Lust for another man's wife is what you had in your eye."

"It wasn't like that, and you know it." Gabriel was definitely getting on Shane's nerves. He needed this last night to forget the responsibilities waiting for him at the little farm on the outskirts of town.

"Do I? And how would I know that? I can only go by what I—along with the whole town—saw."

"Look, Gabriel. We're both tired from our trip. Why don't you head on over and secure a couple of rooms at the hotel while I unwind a bit? I'll catch up with you later."

"I'm not leaving you here, Shane. I'll just stand here and wait."

Shane managed to tamp down his groan. He turned around to hide his frustration. He closed his eyes and analyzed how to get Gabriel to give him a moment's peace.

"There are mirrors everywhere in here, Shane. I can see your expression. And I'm still not leaving."

"Suit yourself."

Shane had already garnered the attention of two pretty ladies who now headed his way.

"Can we get you anything, handsome?"

"A bit of good luck with my card game." Shane crooked his arms, and they each grabbed hold. He worked his way over to a table where three men played a round of poker. Gabriel trailed along. "Y'all have room for one more?"

"You ever played before?"

He shrugged. "A couple of times."

"A couple of times, you say?" The men exchanged glances that insinuated they had a greenhorn joining their game.

"Yes, sir."

"What about your friend there?"

"He doesn't play."

"Good enough for me. Have a seat."

Shane slid into the fourth chair, and the pretty saloon girls stood on either side of him, tussling for the closest spot. Tomorrow might bring a whole slew of headaches into Shane's life, but from where he sat at the moment, life looked pretty good.

two

"Lydia, that nice young man hasn't exited the saloon yet." Bea gawked out the front window of Thompson's General Store, almost tipping over from her awkward angle as she tried to see the front of the saloon down the way. "If you hurry, dear, you might be able to arrange another *tête-à-tête* on the walkway."

Mavis snorted. "Ignore her, Lydia. She's been reading French literature again. The endeavor always gives her new words to try out and fills her head with silly romantic notions. Why she thinks any of it would be of use to us here in the Georgia wilds is surely beyond my understanding."

"I'm standing right here, Mavis. I can peer out the window and hear at the same time."

"I just don't understand why you'd waste your time that way. The time spent on those books is purely a waste."

"Educating your mind is never a waste, Mave, dear. Letting your mind languish is a waste."

Hiding her smile, Lydia glanced away from the bolts of fabric she'd been perusing and looked over at the sisters. "I'm afraid it doesn't bode well for the man's character, Bea, if he's still in the saloon. Surely it doesn't take this long to settle a man in his chair."

"Perhaps the inebriated gentleman put up a struggle. Your knight in shining armor might be in need of assistance himself at this very moment."

"My knight?" Lydia glanced over at Wyatt and lowered her

voice. The boy sat by the door and sucked his peppermint stick, but his hearing tended to be quite sharp, even when it seemed he wasn't paying attention. "I believe he saved us all from being plowed down during that horrible skirmish."

"But he only had eyes for you."

"Nonsense." Lydia turned back to her shopping.

She needed to pick out the fabric for Natalie's birthday dress and finish tallying her purchases. She'd spent too much time in town as it was. She found delicate pink linen that suited Natalie's fair complexion and pulled it from the shelf.

"That's a beautiful fabric," Mrs. Thompson said as she came around the counter near the back of the store.

Lydia ran her fingers over the fine cloth. "It is. It's for my sister's birthday. She'll love it."

"I'm sure she will." The woman made quick work of cutting and packaging the material and other supplies Lydia requested.

"I also need the same amount of your finest white silk."

Mrs. Thompson stopped and looked at Lydia. She peered over her glasses and smiled, an act that softened her features. "Is there a wedding on the horizon?"

Lydia blanched. She surely hoped not. Her stepfather had stepped up his comments pertaining to Lydia's own approaching birthday that hovered on the far-too-close horizon. He'd insisted on the white silk for Natalie, a special eighteenth-birthday surprise, he'd said, but the move seemed much too calculated, even for him.

She almost canceled the request for the silk. It was true enough that they attended the expected parties at neighboring plantations, always the perfect little family. But the white silk was far too rich for even the fanciest of their neighbors' soirees.

Lydia heard the door open and close, but didn't bother to

turn around. The last thing she needed was to get drawn into another conversation that would cause her a further delay. The plantation and its myriad of chores awaited them, and her stepfather didn't appreciate tardiness.

"Here's your parcel, honey." Mrs. Thompson handed over the brown paper-wrapped package. Lydia sighed with relief. "William already loaded your other supplies on your wagon. Anything else I can get for you?"

"No, thank you." Lydia looked around for Wyatt. He wasn't in his chair. He must have dropped down to play on the floor. She smiled at the proprietor and headed for the front of the store. "Wyatt? We need to get going, sweetheart."

No response.

"Wyatt, Daddy's expecting us. We need to get home."

His peppermint stick lay abandoned on the floor by the wooden chair, but Wyatt wasn't anywhere in sight. With a sigh, she picked up the candy and glanced around. She didn't want to rush back to the plantation any more than he did, but they really needed to be on their way.

She tamped down her frustration. At the tender age of six, he didn't understand all the complexities that came along with a trip to town. She made sure of it. She'd have to play along. She began their signature game of hide-and-seek.

"I wonder where Wyatt could be." She peeked around shelves and under tables stacked with goods as she walked toward the back of the store. Mrs. Thompson had returned to the back room, leaving Lydia alone with Beatrice and Mavis. The two women huddled near the front of the store, talking quietly.

Lydia's heart picked up pace as she neared them with few hiding places left and no Wyatt in sight. She remembered hearing the door open and realized no new patron wandered amidst the dry goods.

"Bea? Mavis? Have you seen Wyatt?"

Mavis smiled. "Why yes, dear, he wandered outside just a few minutes ago."

And you thought I was playing hide-and-seek by myself for the fun of it? Lydia seethed. She knew the two spinsters had no experience with small children, but surely even they knew it wasn't safe for a young boy to wander around the walkway without proper supervision.

"Thank you." Lydia pasted on a smile and forced the words through clenched teeth. "Have a good evening."

"You, too, dear."

Lydia exited the store and clutched the parcel with one arm. Stray strands of hair blew across her face, and she held them back with her free hand. Wyatt wasn't anywhere in sight. She could hear the early evening ruckus from the saloon, but other than that, the town was pretty quiet. She glanced back at the saloon. What if Wyatt had gone in search of his newest hero?

She shivered. *Surely not.*

But if not, where else would her little brother have gone?

❧

Shane held his cards close to his chest and tried not to gloat. Finally, he held the perfect hand. The one he'd been waiting for since he'd entered the establishment. After too many thrown games, he now held the coveted royal flush. It wasn't often his cards aligned so perfectly and at such an opportune time.

He debated how to pursue his win. He'd pretend beginner's luck was on his side, he'd play the cards, and then he'd collect his winnings and head over to the hotel to call it an early night.

Shane grinned up at Gabriel. His friend had been shifting

from one foot to the other and sighing for the better part of the hour they'd been here. He'd be more than happy to be on their way. Gabriel glared back at Shane. Or perhaps not. He'd have been happier not to have entered the place he referred to as "the devil's den" in the first place.

"Shane, we really need to go."

"In a minute. Let me play one more hand."

"No, Shane. Now."

"Oh, c'mon, let him play his cards." The fidgety man across the table from him obviously enjoyed the fact that Shane had lost every hand he'd played so far. It would serve the man right when Shane won the round, a win that would be followed by Gabriel's customary lecture about tricking innocent men. As if any innocent men would be playing cards in the saloon.

Shane knew what Gabriel was up to. Gabriel was trying his best to prevent Shane from playing his winning hand and taking all the money. But it wasn't like Shane was cheating. He'd played fair and square. He just hadn't played his best. Until now.

He forced a yawn.

"I'm tired. I think I'll finish things up by betting it all." Shane prepared to push his remaining chips into the center of the table, then hesitated. "I think I'll give it all up."

"You're well on your way," one of the men said under his breath. The other two snickered. Shane pretended not to hear.

"Shane, Savannah's waiting for you to come home."

He ignored Gabriel, too.

"Savannah?" One of the women who'd been draped over his shoulder jumped to her feet, planting her hands on her hips.

The other followed suit. "You have a girl waiting for you at home? I didn't figure you for the type."

"Two girls, actually." Gabriel's tone was entirely too smug. "Both sweet little things, anxiously awaiting his return."

"*Two* girls?" The redhead hit Shane's arm.

He rubbed it with his free hand. For such a little thing, she could pack a punch.

"So you sent that family man home for getting in a ruckus, but then you decided to come in yourself." The brunette tossed her hair.

"They don't mind that I'm here. Why should you?"

The women gaped and shook their heads in unison.

"You're despicable." They turned as one and stalked off toward the back room.

"It's not what you think, ladies." Shane narrowed his eyes at Gabriel as the women stomped away. He called after them, "They're just young'uns. They really don't care that I stopped by!"

Gabriel had the audacity to chuckle. "I don't think you're helping matters, Shane."

"Let's just finish up this round and be on our way, shall we?"

"If you say so." Gabriel seemed more than happy to wait now that he'd disrupted Shane's pleasant camaraderie with the ladies. Gabe hugged his Bible tight—the faded words HOLY BIBLE facing out toward Shane—his lips moving in silent prayer. The other men continued to ignore the dark, soft-spoken man as they had for the better part of the past hour.

"You first," the shifty man said. "You were going for the win?"

Shane drew the moment out. This was the part of the game he enjoyed most. The three men at the table positively glowed with their excitement, mentally counting their winnings as they waited. He'd feel guiltier for duping them if they weren't so giddy at doing the same to a man they considered a beginner. Shane couldn't wait to see the shocked looks that would fill their features when he played his perfect winning hand.

"Me first, huh?" He stalled, hand on chips. "Alrighty then. Let me think a moment."

The other men leaned in, practically panting at the pile of chips about to be thrown.

"I *think* this is a good hand. . .but maybe I should wait and play one more before putting it all in. . . ."

"Don't hold off on our account," Shifty said.

"Well—" Shane drummed his fingers on the table, one breath away from making his play. He felt something brush against his arm.

"Ace, king, queen, jack, and ten!" a small voice shouted from next to Shane's left elbow. "That's a really great hand, mister!"

"Argh!" Shane's garbled words stuck in his throat as he spun around to see the young, towheaded lad from the walkway standing beside him—the one who'd clung to his mother's skirts before Shane had entered the saloon. "What are you doing in here? *Where* is your mother?"

"Dead." The boy stated matter-of-factly. "Where's yours?"

"Dead," Shane spat out. "But that's beside the point. I'm an adult. My mother doesn't travel with me."

"Then I guess I'm a 'dult, too, cause my mama don't travel with me, neither."

Shane forced a strained smile and looked over at the gamblers. "Kid doesn't know his aces from his twos, but he's an adult." He turned back to the wisp of a boy and sent him a pointed look. "Go along now and play outside. The saloon isn't the place for a kid."

"I thought you said the saloon ain't a place for a family man."

"It isn't."

"I'm confused."

"It doesn't matter. What matters is you shouldn't be in here. Now go. Scat."

The boy scowled. "I don't wanna."

"Well, you're gonna." Shane shook his head. Now he was talking like the kid. Shane carefully laid his cards on the table, face down, and snagged the boy by the collar. "Come along."

The boy futilely swung his arms. "I wanna watch you play cards."

"And I wanna watch you walk out that set of swinging doors. Now."

"No."

"Yes."

"You can't make me."

"Wanna bet?"

"Really? You mean it?" The boy's eyes lit up. "Like you was gonna bet with those three men?"

"No." Shane lifted the boy by his overall straps and held him in midair, his small body dangling two feet off the ground. The boy sent him a childish grin. Shane ignored it. "Now you gonna leave?"

"I can't. My feet don't reach the floor." He gave a few halfhearted kicks, which made him swing like a puppet in Shane's hands.

Shane lowered him until he was almost touching the rough-hewn planks below his feet. "There. Now I'm going to put you down, and you're going to get on back to whoever should be watching you."

"No!" The boy gave a well-aimed kick, and Shane dropped

him the rest of the way to the floor with a groan.

"Why you little. . ." He sank into his chair, but still managed to reach out and snag the kid by the overalls again. "Now you listen here—"

"No, *you* listen to *me*!" The pretty blond from outside the store appeared beside him, furious. "Get your slimy hands off my little brother."

"Hey, he started it." Shane kept his grip on the boy's overalls with one hand. He held his other hand up in a gesture of innocence.

"And I'm finishing it." Two bright spots of red colored her cheeks. The heightened color made her eyes appear greener than ever. She was even prettier when angry than she had been when out on the walkway.

Shane shook off the ridiculous thought. "I can explain."

"No need. Just unhand my brother, and we'll be on our way."

"Your *brother* just cost me the card game."

"I couldn't care less," she stated, nose in the air. "Serves you right for indulging in such a foolish and wasteful endeavor. Come along, Wyatt."

Wyatt dug in his heels. "But, Lydie!"

"*Now.*" She tried to drag him out.

"Listen—Miss Lydie—" Shane held tight, wanting compensation.

The woman glared.

Shane narrowed his eyes and settled in. He'd stand his ground until the woman offered a solution to even things up. Truth be told, he didn't want compensation. He was enjoying their little standoff, and he wanted a few more moments of her company. She was mad as a wet hen. He tipped back in his chair with a cocky smile and pulled the boy close, resting an arm on the boy's bony shoulder. He whispered in an aside. "Your sister sure is a spitfire. You know that, Wyatt?"

"How's this for a spitfire?"

The words had barely cleared his mouth when her foot swung out and clipped the back leg of his tipped chair, knocking the legs clean out from under him.

Shane fell to the floor, flat on his back, before he knew what hit him. Speechless, he lay in shock, stunned and staring, as a look of horror crept across her delicate features.

Wyatt had fallen to the floor along with Shane, and a deep belly laugh rose from within him. The rest of the patrons were already laughing when Shane joined in. The little boy's mirth was contagious.

Lydie's blush went from bright red to deep crimson. "If we're through here, I'll be on my way. Wyatt. Come along. Immediately." She spun on her heels and headed for the door.

Gabriel helped Shane to his feet. Shane tugged Wyatt up beside him and hurried in her wake.

"Lydie. Miss—I'm sorry, I don't even know your last name."

"And I'd like to keep it that way," she spat over her shoulder. "There's no need whatsoever for you to know my last name. Wyatt?"

"I'm here, Lydie." Obviously a smart boy, Wyatt hurried forward and grabbed her hand without a backward glance.

"For what it's worth. . .I'm truly sorry for what happened back there."

She didn't acknowledge him or give any indication that she'd heard his heartfelt apology. Shane stood in the middle of the road, feeling bereft as she walked away.

Gabriel appeared beside him. "She really got to you, huh? I've never seen you so taken by a woman."

Shane didn't respond.

Gabriel looked from Lydie to Shane and back. "If it makes you feel any better, the men said that was the best entertainment they've had in a long time and they'd share the winnings with you if you want to go back inside and claim them."

Shane didn't take his eyes off Lydie's retreating back. He watched as she loaded Wyatt in a wagon at the far end of the street, climbed up beside him, and turned the corner to ride out of sight.

three

Lydia tossed and turned, but she couldn't settle down enough to sleep. The trip to town had unnerved her, especially her altercation with the man from the saloon. She couldn't get him out of her head, even after finding out what a scoundrel he really was. Mavis and Beatrice thought him the perfect gentleman, bless their hearts. Lydia was glad they'd still been in the store when she had her exchange with the man.

A noise from the hallway interrupted her musings. She rose up on her arm and tilted her head to listen. The movement disrupted her covers, and cool air slithered underneath her blankets, causing Lydia to shiver. The fire in the hearth on the opposite side of the room had died down to embers, leaving the bed chamber's air chilly.

The floor squeaked outside her door, just before the doorknob turned and the door inched open.

"Lydie?" Wyatt's quiet whimper drifted through the silence.

"I'm here." Lydia wondered if he'd had another nightmare. "Come on in."

She hoped Joseph hadn't heard Wyatt in the hall.

The door opened some more, and she heard the shuffle of Wyatt's feet as he hurried to her bedside. "I'm cold."

The full moon highlighted his slight figure. Lydia lifted the covers. "Climb in bed with me. We'll keep each other warm."

"I had a bad dream." Wyatt's voice dropped to a whisper. "And I'm wet."

His shame carried through the space separating them.

"Oh sweetie. No wonder you're cold. Let's get you dressed in a dry gown." She reached over in the dark and felt around for the gown she kept nearby for him. "We'll get you fixed right up."

"I'm sorry."

Lydia's heart broke for her little brother. His father had humiliated him into thinking he was somehow at fault for soiling his bedclothes at night. Lydia knew the opposite was true. Her stepfather's harsh nature caused Wyatt's nighttime terrors and frustrations.

She made quick work of getting him freshened up and into dry clothes. She pulled back the bedcovers, and he hurried to slip under them. She slid in beside him, allowing him the warm spot where she'd lain several minutes earlier. His shivering stopped after a few moments, and he snuggled close as she tucked them both securely into her bed.

"Let's both try to get some sleep now."

As soon as the words left her lips, a bright light illuminated the hallway. Lydia whispered a quick prayer, knowing what would happen next. As expected, the bedroom door slammed open. Her stepfather filled the doorway. He held up his lantern, leaned against the frame, and leered at her.

"Isn't this a cozy sight? I wonder what could possibly bring young Wyatt running to your bedside."

Wyatt's shivers returned, this time from fear. His tiny body quaked as he pushed closer against her. Lydia placed a reassuring hand against his leg. "He's fine. He just had a nightmare."

"A nightmare, huh?" Never one to wait for an invitation, her stepfather walked farther into the room. He snagged Wyatt's wet nightclothes with his toe and kicked them up into Lydia's face. "Then why is *this* lying on the floor?"

Lydia had a hard time not hating the man. "Please don't do this. Let's let Wyatt go to sleep."

"Don't do what?" His words slurred. He'd been drinking, as usual.

"You know exactly what I'm talking about." Lydia fought to keep the anger from her words. It didn't do any good to provoke him.

"If we can't talk about the boy," he laughed, "then why don't we talk about us."

It was Lydia's turn to shiver. "There isn't any 'us.'"

His crazed laugh filled the room, and Wyatt began to cry.

"There will be soon enough. I noticed you bought the fabric for your wedding dress this afternoon. You'll look mighty pretty in that fancy white silk."

Lydia felt like she was going to be sick. "You told me to buy the fabric for Natalie's birthday."

"That I did. Brilliant, don't you think? I knew if I told you what it was really for, you'd never oblige."

"You're right. And I'm still not going to oblige."

He reached out and grabbed her arm. He jerked her upright to a sitting position in the bed. "You *will* oblige me. Our wedding will be right after your twenty-first birthday. I've waited long enough."

"It's not right. You were married to my mother."

"And your mother is dead. You're no kin of mine. I can marry you if I choose."

"I have no say in the matter?"

"None whatsoever."

"And what if I refuse?"

"Is that what you're doing?" He jerked her arm and squeezed. She'd have bruises in the morning. "Are you *refusing* me?"

"I am." Her voice came out as a whisper, but she had to say it.

He laughed again. "Do you really think you have a choice? You will marry me. And since you have such a disrespectful attitude, I'll move our wedding day up. You'll become my bride first thing in the morning."

Lydia panicked. "No."

"Yes." He released her arm, then shoved her back on the bed. He stalked to the door, but couldn't leave without one more caustic comment to his son. "Enjoy your last night sleeping with your sister, Wyatt. From now on you'll deal with your soiled clothes and your nightmares alone. I won't have you in my bed."

He slammed the door as he went out. Darkness surrounded them.

"Lydie?"

"I'm here, sweetheart." She pulled Wyatt close and closed her eyes, resting her cheek against his baby-soft hair and savoring his little-boy scent. How could someone so precious be related to someone so evil?

"What are we gonna do?"

Lydia sighed. "I don't know."

"You'd make a good mama."

"Thank you, Wyatt. You know I love you with all my heart. Being your mama wouldn't make me love you any more because I already love you with everything I have."

Wyatt giggled. "I know."

"I'm the happiest big sister in the world because I have you."

"And I'm the happiest little brother in the world because I have you." Her little brother finished out the routine with a yawn.

Wyatt's security was the sole reason that almost tempted Lydia to marry the despicable man. But she knew if she married him, nothing would change for the better, and everything would change for the worse.

"Wyatt?"

"What?" His tired voice came out a whisper.

"Things might get rough for a while. But no matter what happens, I want you to be strong. All right?"

"Aw' right."

"I might have to leave for a few days. If I do, I'll come back for you."

"I don't want you to leave!" His voice rose in pitch, and he clung to her.

She held him tight against her. "I don't want to leave, either, but if I do, Natalie and Nathan will be here to watch over you. If you have a bad dream or anything, go to one of them. I need you to be strong."

"Okay."

"Promise me?"

"If you promise me you'll come back."

"I will."

Lydia rubbed his back until Wyatt's soft sobs turned into steady breaths of deep sleep. She needed to figure out a way to avoid the wedding. She could take Wyatt and leave, but where would she go? What would happen to her other siblings? The twins would probably do fine. They'd be eighteen in a few weeks. Nathan would take care of Natalie.

But where would Lydia go? Perhaps Mavis and Beatrice would take them in, but that would only be a temporary fix. Word would get out soon enough that Lydia had taken Wyatt without his father's permission, and she'd be forced to return him. Joseph put on a good front when it came to dealings with the community. It was very unlikely anyone would ever believe her.

Joseph hadn't been this way when her mother had first married him, at least not that he'd let on. But as the years went by, they'd begun to see another side to him. When the war ended, he refused to comply with the mandatory release of his slaves. He kept several of the men in shackles in the barn and outbuildings and used the well-being of their loved ones to keep them compliant.

Lydia began to pray, and immediately Ben came to mind. She hated to put his family in jeopardy, but she knew he'd come through for her. She could release Ben, and he could go for help. He had connections with other freed slaves, and she knew he was in the process of arranging for his own release.

But the wedding was tomorrow. She didn't have any more time. If they worked together, perhaps she and her siblings could go away with Ben tonight. They'd have to take Sadie, Ben's wife, along, too. It would be too dangerous to leave her behind. Her hopes sank. They'd make a large entourage in their quest for escape. Not the best of plans, but she had nothing else in mind.

Lydia waited until she was sure Wyatt had fallen into a deep sleep before slipping out of bed. She donned the outfit she'd worn to town, pulled on thick wool leggings, and laced up her boots. She threw a warm wrap over her shoulders before making her way silently down the long upper hall. Her stepfather's loud snores drowned out any noise she created. She made her way through the lower level of the house and stepped into the kitchen. It took her a moment to locate the key to Ben's shackles and remove it from its hiding place. She clasped it tightly in her hand. A moment later she slipped through the back door and stepped out into the cold night air.

Her boots crunched on the frozen ground as she made her

way to the barn. Ben was highly regarded by the other slaves. To counteract any chance of rebellion, Joseph kept him separated from them. The looming structure looked sinister in the darkness. Lydia ran her hand along the rough wood until she came to the entrance. The large door squeaked loudly as she carefully tugged it open.

"Who's there?" Ben's deep voice called through the darkness.

"It's me, Ben. Lydia. I'm in trouble."

"Get out of the cold, child, and close the door." Ben's chains clanked as he closed the gap between them. "What kind a trouble you in, girl? You and me both be in a heap o' trouble if the master finds you out here wit' me."

"I know, Ben, and I'm sorry to drag you into this. It's just that I don't have any other options."

"What you need me to do?"

Lydia wanted to hug the man. He'd been her ally since she first moved to the plantation, and she knew she could trust him now. "Joseph just announced that he intends to marry me tomorrow." The words rushed out on a sob. "I can't marry him, Ben."

"Of course ya can't. What we gonna do 'bout it? Do ya have a plan?"

"No. I know you've been making plans, and I'm hoping you can take us along with you. Just me, Wyatt, Natalie, and Nathan."

"The plans aren't fully in place, Miss Lydie, and that'd be quite a group."

"I know, but maybe you could hurry the plans along? We could all leave now. I'll sneak back in and get the others." She was pleading now. "Please, Ben."

"Let me think." Ben shuffled back and forth in the darkness between them. "Joseph will come after us if we take your kin. Especially if we wuz to take Wyatt. You have no right to him."

"We can't leave him behind. Joseph doesn't care about him, and you know it."

"He takes pure pride in his ownership, Miss Lydie. I can attest to that."

"I know, Ben."

"Joseph'll make an issue if we takes Wyatt, sure as he'll throw charges 'gainst me."

"He has to find us first." The first ray of hope shot through Lydia. "Stop pacing. I brought the key to unlock your shackles. Let me release them."

Ben froze in place. Lydia felt her way through the darkness and dropped to her knees. She reached forward and felt her way along the cold steel of his chains. She hated her stepfather for treating Ben this way. She felt a certain satisfaction in rebelling against Joseph.

"Ya do realize what'll happen to us if we gets caught, Miz Lydie—to all of us if ya bring your kin along."

Ben's dire words hung in the air.

"It's a risk I'm willing to take. Staying here is no longer an option." She hesitated. "But I don't want to drag you into my mess unless you're sure, Ben."

"My days be numbered, too. I might as well go along with ya." It was his turn to hesitate. "They took my Sadie away earlier this afternoon, Miz Lydie. Master Joseph done sent her away."

"Sadie? No. I saw her before I went into town."

"And after ya left, Master Joseph had a visitor, and that visitor left with my Sadie. She sat in his wagon, tears rollin' down her face. I couldn' do nothin' 'bout it."

"Are you sure?" Lydia's heart sank. Sadie worked for them

in the kitchen. She'd made their breakfast that morning. As long as Ben did as he was told, Joseph left them both alone. "Why would he let Sadie go? Maybe she's gone off to help someone in need."

"I don't know why he'd let her go unless he somehow got wind of my plans. But she be gone for sure. She don't cry like that 'cause she's off to help someone in need. He done knowed about my plans."

"He'd have made an example of you if he did." Another shiver rocked Lydia's body. "But with Sadie gone, you have nothing to lose by leaving."

"That be true, Miz Lydie."

"I'm going for the others. We'll meet you back here." Lydia headed for the door. "Be careful, Ben."

"I be careful and then some, Miss Lydie. You be careful, too."

Even though Lydia inched the door open this time, it still creaked loudly.

"Lydia?" Her stepfather's voice bellowed across the yard.

Terror moved through Lydia.

"Ben, go lie down and pretend to be asleep. I'll act like I was just going in, not leaving. If I don't come back down with the others in thirty minutes, go for help on your own."

"Lydia!" Her stepfather yelled. "I hear you over by the barn."

"I'm here, Joseph."

Ben's chains clanked as he gathered them up, then he rustled his way back to his sleeping area at the back of the barn. She heard his soft snores as her stepfather drew near.

"What do you think you're doing out here in the dark? You think you can get away from me?"

The moonlight shone down and distorted his angry face.

He looked more menacing than ever.

"And leave Wyatt and the others behind? Do you really think I'd do that?"

"Then what are you doing out here, sneaking around in the dark?"

"I heard a noise and came out to investigate."

"What made the noise?"

"I don't know. It must have been the animals. All seems well from what I can see."

Joseph stepped closer to the slightly open door. They could hear Ben's snores loud and clear.

"Get yourself on back inside."

"Yes, sir." Lydia forced her tonality to be civil and hoped he saw her obedience as acquiescence. She took a few more steps. Suddenly the rough hands of one of Joseph's men grabbed her from behind. Lydia fought but couldn't get free. Her stepfather's harsh laugh sounded from a few feet away.

"How stupid do you think I am, Lydia?"

Lydia froze. She was sure the question was rhetorical, though she longed to answer in full honesty.

Instead she hedged. "I'm afraid I don't know what you mean."

"You know exactly what I mean. You have no intention of marrying me in the morning. You're sneaking around out here trying to find a way out of our nuptials."

All coherent thought fled from Lydia's mind. "No—I—"

He slapped her hard against the face.

She whipped her head up and glared at him. "Fine, so what if I was? You can't make me marry you against my will. The preacher will never allow it."

Joseph's face was full of hatred.

"Fine. We won't marry."

It was too easy. He never gave in without punishment.

"What are you going to do?"

"I'm giving you your freedom."

Maybe she'd misread him. Maybe he had some decency left in him after all.

"My freedom?"

"Yes. Your freedom. I'm sending you away. I'll marry Natalie instead. I'm sure she'll be much more open to the idea than you were, once she hears what happened to you when you refused me."

"Why you evil, hateful. . ." Lydia fought hard against the hands that held her. "I hate you."

The person behind her jerked hard, making her teeth rattle and slam down on her tongue. She tasted blood.

Joseph laughed at her. "The feeling is mutual."

She lowered her head. She couldn't let him send her away like this. She needed to protect her siblings. "Fine. I'll stay. I'm sorry. I'll marry you. Please." Lydia's voice sounded panicked, even to her own ears. "Please. Give me another chance."

He waved her off. "Too late. Do what you want with her, boys, but get her as far away from here as possible before dumping her body. I have no further need for the girl."

four

"If you had listened to me and headed for the cabin last night, Shane, you wouldn't have lost all that money at the saloon," Gabriel scolded. "And you wouldn't have had to pay for the hotel. We'd be eating breakfast with your sisters and making our plans for the day."

He'd been yammering about Shane's choice ever since they'd left the hotel an hour earlier.

"And we'd have spent a long, chilly night on the hard, cold floor of the cabin," Shane threw back over his shoulder. "Or worse, we'd have slept in the barn with the horses and the cows. Wasn't the expense for a hotel room worth it for that? Now we've had a good night's sleep, and we're fresh to deal with the girls. We need to figure out where to place them next."

Gabriel shook his head. "I still don't understand why you won't settle down and raise Lucy and Savannah on your own."

"For the hundredth time, Gabriel, I'm not meant to be a family man. Haven't I seen that proved time and again? I lost my parents, my fiancée set her sights on another man and ran off with him, the war took both my brothers—trust me, the girls are better off with a loving family than they are with a bitter old brother like me."

"Better off? They're so unruly and resentful at being left that they get sent away from every home you place them in so you'll come back for them. They're both determined to fight for your love and affection and security. They want to be with you. And you're hardly old."

"I feel like I am. I know you fancy the idea of me raising the girls, but it's not gonna happen, Gabe. You—along with Savannah and Lucy—might as well accept that as fact. As soon as I figure out the girls' next placement, I'll be on my way. Alone."

"Oh no you don't. You aren't going to leave me behind."

"Watch me."

"You've tried to lose me over and over through the years and haven't ever succeeded. You don't want to leave me behind. I think it's time you realize you depend on me."

"I depend on you? You follow my heels at every turn, making my life—" Shane's voice stopped abruptly as they topped the hill that led to the cabin.

"Making your life what, Shane?" Gabriel, a few paces behind him, couldn't see what Shane saw.

Shane yanked his horse to a standstill, speechless, as Gabriel rode up beside him. The scene in the valley set his stomach to churning. His breath came in quick gasps as he tried to take it all in.

"Shane?" Gabriel looked from Shane's horror-struck expression to the ruins that lay before them.

"The girls. The cabin. This is my fault." Small wisps of smoke rose from the burned rubble that had once been the house where his sisters had lived. "I could have prevented this."

"Shane."

"No." The tortured word slipped past Shane's lips. "What have I done? You're right. We could have been here last night, just like you said. That's fresh damage. If we had come last night, we could have saved them. Surely God wouldn't take my sisters, too."

"Maybe they're in the barn."

Shane took off at a hard gallop, leaving Gabriel to follow

behind. He headed straight for the barn, calling Savannah's name. As he neared the open door, he yanked hard on the reins and hit the ground at a run. He entered the eerie quiet of the barn.

"Vannah?" An unnatural silence met his ears, dashing his hopes and confirming his worst fears. "The animals are gone."

"Maybe Maria took them to a neighbor's after the fire started."

"Always the optimist, aren't you, Gabriel? Look around you. Does it look like they cleared out and went to a neighbor's? Would they have abandoned the farm like this?" Shane stalked toward the skeletal remains of the cabin. "I suppose they loaded up their chickens and cows and horses and took them along with them while the house burned down. Why would they do that, knowing they'd be back to try to salvage the house? Where are the neighbors? Wouldn't they have come right over to help?"

Gabriel stood silent and let Shane lash out. His eyes reflected Shane's heartache.

"Where else would the animals be, Shane? They didn't get out on their own."

The acrid stench of burned lumber blew toward them on the breeze. Shane moved closer.

Gabriel touched his arm. "Don't, Shane. Let me."

"No, it's my fault. I want to look in the face of the damage I've caused."

"It's not your fault."

Shane froze in place and watched his friend walk toward the debris. He tried to convince himself that the burning sensation behind his eyes was caused by the blowing ash.

He clenched his hands. He reared his head back and roared. "Lucy! Savannah!"

Gabriel jumped, but no childish voices responded. Gabriel continued his trek into the debris.

Shane shook his fist at the sky. "You did this to me! Why? One miracle, is that so much to ask? I just need one chance for things to go right."

Fact was, Shane hadn't wanted the girls, and God had taken them away. Shane had chance after chance to care for them, and he'd chosen to place them anywhere but in his own protective care. It was his fault, not God's. He hadn't even said good-bye the last time he'd left them.

Lucy always cried and hung on his hem while Savannah gave him the silent treatment when he'd prepare to leave. They'd wanted to be with him, and selfishly he'd convinced himself that he needed to earn their keep by gambling, an occupation that didn't allow him to drag along two small girls. The last time he'd left, he'd snuck out in the middle of the night in order to avoid the tantrums.

If he could do it all again, he would do things so much differently. He'd stay with them. He'd find a way to be the man they needed him to be.

"Shane. There's something over here you need to see."

Shane's stomach churned. He didn't want to see whatever Gabriel had to show him, but he deserved it. While he'd lain all cozy in the warm, soft bed at the hotel, his sisters had faced—this inferno.

He sluggishly moved forward. "What is it?"

"Nothing."

"You called me over to see nothing?"

"I don't see any—remains."

"Maybe the fire burned too hot."

"I don't think so. Everything else is here, charred, but intact. The bed frame, the dressing table, the kitchen table.

A hot fire would have reduced it all to dust."

Shane saw something pink by the wood box. A small, simmering pile of rubble on the far side of the cabin popped. He walked over and picked up the pink-clad object. He started to laugh, the sound harsh. "Lucy's doll."

The smoke-damaged doll had survived the fire. The doll he'd brought her as a peace offering the last time he'd seen them. Just before he'd left them with Maria.

"A stupid cloth doll made it through the fire. The wood box full of kindling made it through intact."

He glanced around at all the stray pieces of firewood scattered around the plank floor. "Why didn't this wood catch fire?"

"Looks like the fire blew the other way. It seems to have started in the corner by the bed."

"Lot of good that did the girls."

"Based on the blankets here in the corner nearest the wood box, the girls slept in this corner of the cabin."

"While I slept in my nice hotel bed."

Shane picked up a random piece of wood and flung it forcefully at the wood box. The loud clatter and vibrations caused the wood inside the box to shift.

Gabriel didn't answer. He just stood there, staring at Shane. "We should go."

Shane glared at the wood box. The stupid thing stood there untouched. It should have burned. "Remember when Savannah climbed in the one at home while they were playing hide-and-seek?"

"I do." Gabriel's eyes pleaded for Shane to stop talking and start walking.

Shane knew Gabriel wanted to keep him away from the pain the memories would bring up.

Gabriel took a deep breath. "She was bit by a snake and swore she'd never go near another wood box again."

"She was so sick from the bite. We didn't think she'd make it."

"But she did." Gabriel grinned. "She's a little fighter." His grin disappeared just as quickly as he realized what he'd said. "I'm sorry."

Shane picked up another large piece of wood and threw it at the box. "If she hadn't been so terrified of the snakes, maybe she would have crawled inside and survived."

"Shane—" Gabriel flinched as Shane hurled a third log with all his might at the wooden structure.

Shane didn't care. He picked up two more and hurled them in the same direction before he stalked toward his horse.

He swung up on Pal's back and spurred him into action. He heard Gabriel behind him as he hurried to keep up. Blinding tears flowed freely. He'd made it to the edge of the barn when a piercing shriek stopped him.

At first he thought Gabriel had taken his grief to the extreme, but when Shane spun around, Gabriel looked as startled as he felt.

"Did you hear that?"

Shane nodded. He slid his shotgun from the saddle as Gabriel did the same with his rifle. They turned their horses and rode over to the wood box.

The scream sounded again, louder than before. Shane jumped down and tripped as he scrambled to get back to the wood box. He steadied himself with a hand in the dirt and kept going. Gabriel rode up close behind him. Shane flung the lid open with his free hand and looked down into Savannah's precious, angry, soot-covered face.

Tears coursed through the black, leaving trails down her cheeks. Shane followed the motion of her terrified eyes and saw a piece of wood that resembled a snake, coiled like it was hissing, on the top layer of wood beside her. The wood, knocked off balance when Shane had thrown the logs, had pinned Savannah in place.

"It's okay, sweetheart. Look here, it's just a piece of wood."

Shane quickly dropped his shotgun. He pulled Savannah from the box and hugged her against his chest.

His eight-year-old sister shoved him away. "'Bout time y'all *finally* decided to get here."

A wave of relief rolled through Shane. With her perpetual scowl in place, it seemed Savannah would be just fine. He pulled her close again. "Where's Lucy?"

"Shane. I can't breathe." She struggled to push him away again, her complaint muffled against the front of his shirt.

He relaxed his hold, but didn't let go. Her warm, safe little body felt so good in his arms.

"Lucy's still in there." She pointed behind her toward the wood box. "She's scared."

Shane picked Savannah up and walked over to look into the box.

Lucy lay curled in the farthest corner, motionless, her eyes wide with fear.

Shane kissed Savannah's head before handing her off to Gabriel. Gabriel wrapped her in his arms, his face crinkled with concern. Shane saw the unspoken question in his eyes. *Why wasn't Lucy making some sort of noise? Had she been injured by the falling wood?*

"Luce." Choked up, Shane reached inside for his youngest sister. He gingerly lifted her out, pulling her warm body against him with relief.

"She's alive." He caught Gabe's eye and laughed. "They're both alive, Gabe!"

"So I see." Gabe's smile was every bit as big as Shane's as he hugged Savannah close. Savannah snuggled into her brother's friend's secure embrace, her narrowed eyes following Shane's every move.

"Let's get them over to that tree." Shane motioned toward the large Spanish moss–draped oak tree that grew tall against the barn. "Something isn't right with Lucy. We need to check them both for injuries."

"Shane?"

"Yes, Vannah?"

"Emma's in there, too."

"What?" Shane wasn't sure he'd heard her right. Emma was Maria's four-year-old daughter, same age as Lucy. Savannah had to be mistaken. They'd been through a rough night. He hadn't seen anyone else in the box.

"Emma's still in there, Shane. I could feel Lucy breathing, but Emma didn't move at all. Is she all right?"

Gabriel let Savannah slide to the ground and reached for Lucy. Savannah clung to Gabe's side. Shane handed Lucy over and hesitantly peeked into the wood box. He saw another small body nestled in the closest corner. The only possible way for all three girls to fit was for Savannah to have pushed her way up near the piece of wood that she thought was a snake. Shane had received his miracle. His sisters were safe.

Emma shifted when he touched her.

"It's all right, honey. I'm going to get you out of there."

She didn't respond, and his heart sank. He reached down to pick her up. Her body also felt warm. A bit too warm. He glanced over at Savannah. "She's just sleeping."

Relief filled her eyes. "There wasn't much room. I tried to

get the lid open, but I couldn't." Her tears started again. She angrily swiped at them with the back of her hand.

Shane adjusted Emma in his arms and reached to pull his traumatized sister close. "Let's get out of here."

They guided the girls to the nearby tree and settled them in the grass.

"Did the shifting wood hurt anyone?"

"No." Savannah pushed her dark hair away from her face. "I was closest and kept the little girls below me."

"You did good, Vannah. I'm really proud."

Her blue eyes, so similar to his, stared up at him. Her hesitant smile lit his heart.

Shane glanced over at Emma. "We need to check the little girls, and then I'll look you over, okay?"

"I'm fine."

"All the same, I'll feel better if I make sure."

Savannah nodded.

Gabriel brought over the horses and removed some packages from the saddlebags. "Who wants something to eat?"

With Savannah distracted by the snack, Shane gave the younger girls his full attention. Lucy appeared to be sleeping, but Shane feared she might have been hurt by one of the logs. He carefully removed her clothes and checked her for any signs of bruising. Her too-thin frame bothered him. He threw her soot-covered clothes into a pile and covered her with a blanket.

He did the same with Emma. No signs of a mark on her, either, but she felt a little warm.

"Savannah, has Emma been sick?"

Worry creased Savannah's face. "Yes. She got sick before Maria."

"Maria was sick?"

"Yes."

Shane had to listen close to hear her grief-stricken words.

"I guess I kilt her. I helped Maria take care of Emma, and Emma started to get better. But then Maria got sick, too. I did the same things for her, but she didn't get better. I brought her tea. I made cool cloths for her forehead. But the last two days, she didn't move."

"What happened last night, Van?"

"Some men came. One wanted Maria to marry him, but he wasn't very nice. I was scared. They banged on the door so I made the little girls get in the wood box through the little inside door. Lucy cried, but I told her we had to be quiet and brave. Emma was sleeping so I put her in first, then I got in and thought I heard snakes. I told Lucy I'd get closest to them and protect her. I had her hand, and she dropped her doll. I made her get in without the doll. Lucy got mad at me and didn't talk to me again."

"That's okay, Van. I have the doll. We found it in the cabin."

Savannah's deep blue eyes twinkled. "She'll be happy to know that. You should wake her up and tell her."

"Let's let her sleep a bit longer. I think she's really tired. What happened next after you got in the box?"

"The men banged around a bit. They said Maria was dead and they'd need to bury her. They said they'd split the animals between them. They were banging stuff around and said something caught on fire. Then I thought I heard snakes and was too scared to move."

"Maria's sickness caused her demise, Van. You didn't kill Maria. You kept the little girls safe. That's all that matters."

"I fell asleep and didn't wake up until I heard something banging on the wood box. I think it was giant snakes trying to get us."

"No, Van, I was the one who was banging. That was only me. I thought I'd lost you, and I got angry and threw several logs at the box. I didn't know you were in there. I'm sorry I scared you."

"You didn't know." She shrugged and pinned him with her gaze. "But now that you have us back, you'll have to keep us. Right?"

Shane evaded her question. Savannah narrowed her dark blue eyes and stared him down, a perfect imitation of Gabriel's glare. Gabriel loudly cleared his throat before stomping off to the pump. Now he'd have both of them petitioning him to settle down. Shane turned to Emma.

"Emma." He gently shook the little girl. "Emma, wake up."

Emma opened her eyes, focused, and began to wail. Shane held her close and rocked her until she quieted.

Gabriel returned with a piece of cloth he'd dampened at the pump. "You sure look like a family man to me."

Shane ignored him and cleaned Emma's face before pulling two new dresses and fresh sets of underclothes from one of the packages he'd brought along for the girls—this trip's peace offering. He'd brought the clothes for Lucy, but Emma needed something to wear, too.

"Look here at these pretty dresses, Em. Which one do you like?"

Emma pointed to the light blue dress.

"Vannah, can you come over here and help Emma get dressed while I take care of Lucy?"

Savannah flipped her disheveled hair over her shoulder and eyed the new dresses as she moved to Emma's side.

"I have a package for you, too, Van."

She shrugged. Now that she felt secure, she was going to give Shane her indifferent side. It happened every time he returned. He always arrived bearing gifts, and she always acted like she didn't care.

According to Gabriel, she really didn't care. On the heels of the thought, Gabriel leaned close. "She wants you, not the gifts, Shane."

Shane reached for Lucy. He freshened her up and slipped the pink dress over her head. His large fingers had a hard time fastening the tiny buttons. She could pass as Emma's twin with her blond hair and blue eyes. Eyes he wanted to see right now. He shook her shoulder. "Luce. Wake up."

Lucy shrugged his hand away and burrowed deeper against Shane's chest. He grinned and persisted. "Luce."

She wriggled in his arms and finally opened her eyes and looked up at him. She mouthed his name, but no sound came out.

"You need a drink? Is your throat sore?"

She nodded.

"I'll get her a drink." Gabe was on his feet and hurrying back toward the pump.

She clung to Shane, and he held her close for a few minutes.

"Luce, I'm going to leave you with Gabe and check on Savannah."

Lucy glanced over at Gabriel, who'd arrived with the water, and reached up to cling to Shane.

"I'll ready the horses." Gabriel walked away to give them some privacy.

Savannah looked up from her package of clothes. She yanked her new hairbrush through her tangled hair. "I told you I'm fine."

Shane settled Lucy beside him on the blanket. "I know you did."

With a sigh she scooted closer. Shane held up a blanket,

and she stripped down to her underclothes. He checked her back and neck specifically, still not believing she hadn't been hurt. "There's nothing here."

"I told you."

He wrapped the blanket around her. "Why don't you slip over there to the barn and put on your new clothes? Bring the sooty ones back so we can wash them down the road."

She grabbed her package and scampered off with the blanket held tight around her.

"God gave you your miracle. Are you going to throw it in His face?" Gabriel called out.

"No, I'm not going to throw it in His face, Gabe. I haven't said a thing about what I'm going to do."

"We should go back to town."

Shane contemplated his next words carefully. "I'm thinking we should return to the family homestead."

Gabriel nervously cleared his throat. "The, um, *the* family homestead? As in *your* family homestead?"

"Yes, Gabriel. My family homestead. Who else's homestead would I return to?"

"This is unexpected."

Shane leaned around and looked up at his friend. "You have a problem with us going back? I thought this was what you've been wanting."

"Well, it is. But after all this time I didn't think you'd really consider it."

"What am I missing, Gabe? Is there something I need to know?"

"No. It's just, the house—"

"I know how things grow around here. The house is probably buried beneath a layer of vines. It's not like I expect the house to be as I left it."

Gabriel muttered. "That's an understatement."

"I'm not worried about the house, Gabe. We need a place where we can settle in while we figure out what we'll do next. I want to be with the girls. I still don't feel like I'm cut out to be a family man, but I don't want to leave them."

Their conversation was interrupted by the arrival of a dark, emaciated man.

five

The man's slow, shuffling footsteps were muffled by the dirt road. Gabriel hurried over to help him. His dust-coated bare feet and torn, filthy clothes told of a long journey or at the very least, hard days of neglect.

The man waved him off. "I's a slave from the Maxwell Plantation. I need help searchin' for my mistress. She be in trouble."

Shane and Gabriel exchanged glances.

Gabriel laid a gentle hand on the man's arm. "With all due respect, the war is over and has been for several years. Slavery has been outlawed."

"Tell my owner." The man raised his pant leg and showed the deep scars from years in shackles, some of the abrasions quite fresh.

"That's just wrong." Gabriel's voice shook with outrage.

The man's agitation continued. "I'm Ben. My master done sent my wife away yesterday. Last night, he say he gonna force marriage on his wife's oldest daughter."

"His stepdaughter?" Shane tried to follow the man's frantic words.

The man nodded.

"I take it she wasn't agreeable with the choice of groom?"

"No suh. My master be the groom of choice."

"I see." Shane remembered what happened to his mother after her sorry choice of a spouse. His father had left her alone with Shane and his brothers while he continued his travels on the gambling circuit. He'd returned a total of two times, those two visits producing Savannah and Lucy. After Lucy's birth, they'd never heard from him again. Shane was sure he was cut from the same cloth and hoped he could do right by the girls. "What happened next?"

"She done refused him. She run out in the dark o' night to get my help. She unlocked my shackles, but her father, he caught her."

"He knew she released you?" That didn't bode well. If the man was corrupt enough to keep slaves after the law declared it illegal, he'd not hesitate in correcting his rebellious stepdaughter.

"No. She told a story to divert his attentions. He act like he gonna go along with it, but then two of his men, they grab her, and he send her off wit' them."

Shane's jaw clenched. He didn't sit well with anyone who mishandled a woman or child. "Sent her off where?"

"I dunno, suh. I waited till I wuz sure it be safe, and I came fo' help. You the first people I seen." He glanced at the remains of the smoldering cabin. "And it look like you down on yo' luck, too."

A couple of thoughts warred in Shane's mind. He'd made it clear that he wasn't a family man, nor did he want anyone to rely on him. Despite that fact, he had Gabriel, Savannah, Lucy, and Emma to deal with. Now this man showed up needing help, not only for himself, but for someone else.

Yet Shane couldn't deny he'd been given a second chance with his sisters. If they needed help and he wasn't around, he hoped someone would step in to help them. It only took a moment for Shane to act.

"We only have two horses for six people. It'll be slow going." He looked at the man's weak body and sore feet. "We can take turns riding and walking."

"Or," Savannah piped in for the first time, "we can round up Twister and take him along with us."

"Twister?" Shane motioned toward the barn. "All the animals are gone."

"I doubt Twister is." Savannah's smile quirked up at the corner. "You know how Twister hates strangers. When the men tried to get him last night, I heard one scream that the palomino had bit him. There's no way Twister let that man capture him."

"Twister." Shane grinned. "Ornery old boy. Where is he?"

"Most likely in the trees behind the barn. He never goes far."

"Hurry and round him up, and we'll be on our way."

Savannah's mount was as stubborn as his young owner. They made a great pair, Twister not doing any better with strangers than Savannah. For the first time ever, Shane was grateful for the willful horse's trait.

Gabriel looked at Emma, who now sat quietly on the blanket, watching the men as they talked. He lowered his voice. "What are we going to do with Emma?"

Shane raised a shoulder. "We're taking her with us. What choice do we have? Maria was a widow who had no relatives or close friends. The girls are the closest thing Emma has to family. She's my responsibility as much as the other girls are."

A flash of humor passed through Gabriel's eyes, but the man was smart enough to stay quiet. Shane spun on his heels and went to help Savannah round up her wayward horse.

They made quite a sight as they rode out. Gabriel rode Twister, the cantankerous creature taking up all his attention as they took the lead. Savannah sat beside Shane on the seat of the old buckboard the marauders had left untouched in the barn. Pal, along with some help from Gabriel's horse

Chester, pulled the wagon.

Lucy and Emma curled up on Gabriel's bedroll in the back of the wagon. They quickly dropped off to sleep. Ben rode along with them. The exhausted and emaciated man was in no condition to fight high-spirited horses like Pal and Twister. He let down his guard and settled in. He was asleep almost as quick as the little girls.

Shane sighed as he surveyed the group of people scattered around him.

God, I told You I wasn't worth anything to anyone and I didn't want to be responsible for a family. Yet You've placed one person after the next in my care. I'll do my best to handle things as they are, but I'd be mighty obliged if You'd take these burdens from me as soon as possible.

❧

Lydia had survived the long night, no thanks to her horrible stepfather and his cruel intentions.

She welcomed the stillness and thanked God that a few hours earlier, when the men had dumped her into the brush at the edge of the road, she'd been dumped without the men taking any liberties. She had no idea where she was. When they left the plantation, they'd taken the dirt road that led from the family estate and turned the opposite direction from town. She'd lost track of their travels when they took a fork in the road that led to higher ground. The plan—at least according to their detailed conversation as they traveled—had been for them to toss her off the side of the mountain. A chilly rain pushed their hand, and they'd pulled her off the wagon earlier than expected in their hurry to get back to the plantation.

Lydia felt the cold and was aware that lying here on the damp ground might not be the best idea. But for the moment, she remained there and savored the fact that she was safe and free from the despicable men who had taken her from the plantation.

The breezy morning air permeated the cloth of her dress, and she snuggled deeper into her wrap, a part of her willing the comforting darkness to return while the other part of her knew she needed to go for help and get back to her siblings on the plantation. No way would she leave them in her stepfather's care a moment longer than necessary. An internal prompting to move had her pushing up on her elbows. Her head throbbed. Her eyes squinted against the brightness as she took in her surroundings. The effort was rewarded with shooting pain that cascaded through her temples.

Thick, overgrown trees above her and the partially overcast sky blocked her direct view of the morning sun, preventing her from figuring out the time. Based on the slant, though, she thought it was midmorning. She listened for a moment, suddenly afraid to tarry. What if her stepfather had second thoughts and decided to come back for her? Or maybe he'd send his men back to fetch her. Or worse, perhaps they'd return to make sure their plan had worked and if they found her alive—they'd feel the need to remedy the situation.

Lydia had no idea if Ben had made it off the plantation. He might have decided to reattach the shackles and stay put. She wouldn't blame him if he did. Her situation proved Joseph had no qualms when it came to showing his evil nature.

She needed to find help on her own. She couldn't rely on anyone else. If Ben had managed to safely escape the plantation, her siblings didn't know where she was—and who knew what story Joseph would concoct for them. Nathan was already wary of the man, and if he had any suspicion that

Joseph had orchestrated Lydia's disappearance—Nathan's wrath would equal or surpass Joseph's. She couldn't stand the thought of Nathan getting hurt.

Dear Lord, please keep Joseph away from me as I work my way home. Please watch over Wyatt, Natalie, and Nathan. Please keep Ben safe, too. Protect them all until I can think of a way to help them. Please let me find help and a trustworthy friend—soon.

The whispered prayer uttered under the tranquil morning light brought her a small measure of peace. Lydia couldn't get over the serenity and quiet of the area surrounding her. Even the local creatures were still, her presence putting them on alert.

Her head hurt, and she debated staying in place a bit longer or trying to get up and go for help. The cool air muddled her mind. Or maybe it was the head wound that muddled her thoughts. The wooziness overcame her determination to find help. She closed her eyes and tried to drift off, but thoughts of her stepfather's return prevented sleep from returning.

She pushed to her feet, glad she'd taken the time to pull on the wool leggings before heading out to request Ben's assistance. Though her feet were cold, she wasn't in jeopardy of suffering from frostbite from the early spring night spent out in the elements. She stood on shaky legs and tried to ignore the throbbing in her head and aches and pains of her body.

The men had discussed their choices for her demise in depth and had argued about the best way to go about it, but in the end the dropping temperature, rain, and late hour had won out, and they'd decided to dump her over the side of the road. In the dark they'd chosen the wrong spot, and instead of falling to her demise, she'd only suffered a hard wallop to her head. She'd fought them, and they'd kicked and hit until they were able to push her off the wagon. With a scream, she'd flown backward into the darkness. Her head struck a tree or something just as unforgiving and that was all she remembered until she'd awakened, miraculously alive.

She felt sure God had used the weather conditions to spare her from further abuse and death, and to get her away from Joseph, but her siblings weren't as fortunate. They weren't safe as long as Joseph was with them.

Lydia had to get back to Wyatt and the twins. She had to get home before Natalie's eighteenth birthday. In two short weeks, they'd celebrate, and Joseph would announce his plans. She took a step and stumbled. Dizziness set her head to swirling. She paused, leaning against the rough bark of a nearby tree with a shaky hand.

The gambler's face chose that moment to appear in her thoughts, and she semismiled. He'd seemed so confident on the walkway while taking care of the inebriated man. He'd seemed so thoughtful and charming when he looked her way and winked and left to take the man inside. She'd love to have the aid of someone like him right about now.

Reason pushed that thought away. He'd also snagged her brother by the shirt when Wyatt made him lose his nefarious card game. The scoundrel. Lydia frowned. He hadn't actually hurt the boy. In fact, in light of the seriousness of what Wyatt did, the man had been amazingly patient with her brother. Wyatt thought him the perfect hero. Lydia needed a hero. She needed a knight in shining armor to ride in and save her. The handsome gambler would be perfect for the feat. She sighed and smiled another dreamy smile.

If he were there, she'd swoon and peer into his handsome face. He'd catch her and grin, his smile charming. His long, dark hair would fall into his face, and she'd gently push it away, tucking it behind his ear so she could better see his deep blue eyes.

Lydia put a hand to her head and forced away the irrational musings. Her head wound must be worse than she thought. The last thing she needed was a gambler—an untrustworthy man of any sort—invading her life. And to stand here while her mind wandered wasn't doing anyone any good.

Though Wyatt thought the man was the answer to all life's woes, Lydia knew better. She closed her eyes and leaned her forehead against the tree until the dizziness—and crazy notions—passed.

She pushed herself to carry on. She stepped over roots, slipped on the furry green moss that surrounded them, and pulled her way up the rocky incline until she reached the road. She half crawled onto the unkempt road and stood to survey her situation.

Spanish moss–draped oak trees and huge magnolias flanked both sides of the dirt road that stretched out before her. She didn't see any sign of a cabin or family home in either direction.

A barely discernable trail worked its way through the trees a few yards to her left. She could stay on the main road and hope she picked the right direction to reach the closest dwelling, or she could follow the trail and hope it led to someone's homestead. If she took the road, she could run into Joseph or his men. Though she'd kept track of the switchbacks as well as she could, the beating they'd given her just before they tossed her off the side of the mountain muddled her thoughts. She figured if she headed down the mountain, she'd eventually hit the road that led back to her home.

The protective safety of the brush-surrounded trail won out. Lydia began to hike, holding onto the trees and stopping to rest whenever she felt light-headed. Her entire body ached. Several times she swooned, sure she'd lose consciousness on the trail, but each time she rallied and made her way forward after the dizziness passed. She felt safe and protected as she walked through the wild palmettos, vines, and scrub that were on the verge of overtaking the path.

When she reached the end of the trail, she faced another open road instead of the cabin she'd hoped for. Tears of frustration blurred her vision. She wasn't sure if it was the original road the men had traveled the night before or one of the switchbacks, but it was better than being lost in the woods. Nothing looked familiar. The sun peeked out from behind the clouds and warmed her back.

Lydia had walked downhill the entire time. Chances were it was the same road they'd traveled up into the hills. That is, if they'd zigzagged up the mountain more than if they'd traveled around it. For all she knew, she could be on the far side of the mountain, walking away from home and farther into the wilderness. Panic threatened to overtake her. She forced herself to proceed with the thought she hadn't traveled that far away from home.

She tried to focus. If town was to the west of their plantation, she'd be east of home, based on the original direction they'd taken when leaving. If she was on the right path, she'd need to follow the sun's lead and head west. For now, the sun was directly overhead. She'd have to wait a bit to see which way the sun moved before she'd know which direction she'd need to travel. Of course if the sun didn't move parallel to the roadway, she'd know she was completely and hopelessly lost. She prayed the sun would move parallel to the road. Regardless, the road had to lead somewhere. She'd find her way in time.

Lydia released her breath with that thought and headed over to a soft patch of grass that surrounded a large magnolia. She settled beneath it, letting the sun warm her body through the branches. Her head pounded, and she knew she'd overdone it. The head injury should have taken precedence when she set her pace. She leaned back against the sturdy tree, closed her eyes, and contemplated her choices.

Unbidden, the image of the handsome man from the saloon returned to fill her head. He'd set her heart to fluttering out there on the walkway, there was no denying that. But she apparently had her mother's aptitude when it came to choosing men because the scoundrel had shown another side when she saw him in the saloon. She couldn't keep dwelling on him.

Scowling, she pushed the image away. She didn't need help from a man like him. As a matter of fact, she couldn't think of one single male she'd trust to help her. Most of the men on the neighboring plantations were loyal friends to her stepfather. They'd never believe her story. Frustrated, she tried to come up with a man-free plan. Maybe if she could get Nathan's attention out in the fields, they could work together to come up with a plan. Though he was male, he was trustworthy. If she caught him in the light of day, instead of in a panic in the middle of the night, perhaps he'd be reasonable and not act rashly. Returning to the plantation on her own seemed to be her best option.

Lydia's stomach rumbled, reminding her she hadn't eaten since the day before. She ignored it and tried to focus on her travels.

She felt it best to stick to the road. If Joseph or his men were going to come back to see how she'd fared after last night's venture, they surely would have been there by now. She felt a bit safer taking that route this time around. She didn't want to get caught in the woods later in the day when darkness fell. She'd feel safer sleeping—or at least trying to fall asleep—if she were near the road.

A lizard ran across her ankle, and she stifled her scream. Lizards she could deal with. Snakes she could not. She scoured the surrounding area, making sure no other living creature waited to catch her off guard. The effort distracted her. She wasn't paying attention to her surroundings and didn't hear the arrival of company until they were almost upon her.

Voices carried her way from up the road. In her panic that the newcomers would include Joseph or his hands—and after her past twenty-four hours, she wasn't about to take the time to see who was coming—she looked up and saw the low branches of the tree above her made a perfect climbing perch. She worked her way up into the tree, trying to keep the dizziness at bay, and waited.

six

Shane scanned the road ahead. They needed to take a break. The little girls needed to stretch their legs, and everyone needed to eat. He saw an open grassy patch under a tree just ahead.

He called out to Gabe. "Let's pull off in that grassy spot." He motioned toward the side of the road.

Savannah sighed. "Why're we stopping so soon? There'll be plenty of chances to rest after we get home."

"We won't be long." Shane glanced over at her. "What's your hurry anyway?"

"I just wanna make sure we get there before you go changin' your mind about keepin' us."

"I'm not changing my mind. I have no one else to take you to right now, Van."

"Thanks. That's reassuring." Sarcasm dripped from her words.

"Listen, I'm not going anywhere. God just gave you back to me. I'm not letting you go anytime soon. I'm keeping you. Got it?" He felt her relax and rest her cheek against his arm.

For all her bravado and posturing, she was such a tiny thing. It suddenly dawned on him that when he'd left her behind, she'd been forced to be the strong one for Lucy. She'd picked up where he'd left off, just like their mother had when abandoned by his father.

"You ever realize how much you're like our ma?"

"I hardly remember her." Savannah shrugged. Her next

words, quietly spoken, betrayed her attempt to feign indifference. "In what way? I mean, how d'you suppose I'm like her?"

"Mama had grit. Spunk. She found a way to survive, even when life was hard." And for her, life was always hard.

"What happened to our pa?"

"He didn't stick around long after Lucy was born."

"So I guess that makes you a lot like him."

Her words didn't sit well with Shane. All through the years he'd wondered why card games held so much more power over their father than his desire to be with his loved ones. As soon as Shane was old enough, he'd gone straight out to find the answer. He'd found that he had a knack for cards and learned cards had the same power over him.

Savannah was right. He'd let the cards become more important to him than the little sisters who needed him more than ever without their ma. "I'm sorry, Vannah. I don't want to be like him in that way."

"But our ma, she was a good person?"

"She was." Shane smiled. "She was a very good person. The best. She worked hard to provide for us."

At first he'd assured himself he was only playing the cards so he'd have money to send back to his ma. He'd been able to make her life easier in those last few years. But the cards had taken precedence over everything else. He should have been there for the girls, just as their pa should have been there for their ma.

"You know, if you found us a new ma, you wouldn't hafta be herdin' us all over Georgia."

Savannah's words almost made him fall off the wagon. He choked. "A ma? Where do you get such thoughts?"

"I've been thinkin'. If you found us a ma, we could go home and settle back in."

"We're going home now, Vannah. Isn't that what I've been saying?" Shane reiterated. Again. "And I haven't exactly sent you all over Georgia. Georgia covers a lot of area. Haven't you ever seen a map before? Our little area is only a small part of the whole."

"Sure, I learnt all about maps and Georgia in school." Savannah huffed. "Oh, wait, maybe I haven't learnt about it after all because I ain't never been to school."

Shane cringed. She had a point. He'd moved them around so much he hadn't really given the girls' schooling much thought. Gabriel had pressed him about the importance of Savannah's education a couple of years earlier, but Shane hadn't realized how quickly time had passed. He glanced back at her.

"Your lack of education is obvious in your choice of words. Since when have you used 'ain't' and 'learnt' anyway?"

He arrived at the tree. He jumped down from the wagon and reached up for Savannah. She ignored him and clambered to the ground. Lucy and Emma woke up, reached for Shane, and wandered around after he lifted them to the ground. Gabriel and Ben tended to the horses.

"I guess I learnt it since we lived with Maria. She talked like that all the time. I got used to hearin' it, and I guess I started sayin' it."

"Well, Mama raised you better. We'll work on proper language while we're at the house." And he'd make sure to pick more appropriate caretakers in the future, a feat that would add further challenge to their search.

"*While we're at the house.*" Savannah glared and dropped to a sitting position on the ground. "I knew it wouldn't last."

"We're going home, Savannah. Why can't that be enough? Let's take one day at a time and see what happens." Shane sank down beside her.

"I want to *stay* at home." Savannah's voice broke. "I heard you talkin' to Gabriel. You only plan to settle in long enough to figure out another place to send us."

"It's not practical to keep you with me. I have to work."

"You could find us a ma. She could watch us while you work. You could marry her and could stay home and be our pa. We'd be a family again."

"We're still a family, Van."

"I want a ma."

"And I'm not going to find you one. Settling down like that isn't in my plans, Savannah." A niggling thought made him pause. If he thought about it, planting his feet at home called to his heart. The thought scared him. "Listen, I'm doing the best I can. You're proving the fact I don't have a clue on the best way to raise you."

"If you found us a ma, she'd know how to raise us."

He leaned against the trunk of the tree and stretched his legs out in front of him. He crossed his ankles with an air of nonchalance. He held out his arms. "Fine, Savannah. I'll tell you what. If God wants me to find a wife and make her a ma for you girls, He'll have to drop her on my lap."

"You know that won't happen." Savannah narrowed her eyes and pinned him with a glare. Her nose wrinkled as she growled at him. "Don't make fun of me."

They froze in a standoff of wills. Shane wanted to laugh. His sister couldn't be any more like him in nature. He raised his eyebrow to egg her on, his arms still outstretched. Savannah slapped her arms into a folded position across her chest and resumed her pout.

"Sorry, sis, I guess it isn't meant to be." Shane wiggled his outstretched fingers. "If He'd wanted me to have a wife, she'd surely be here by now."

Savannah looked away.

He closed his eyes. "Are You sure, God? Vannah really wants a ma." He opened his eyes to see Savannah staring at him, her blue eyes questioning his sincerity. He felt a pang of guilt. Gabriel would be so disappointed in him.

I'm sorry, Lord, I didn't mean to be sarcastic or disrespectful. The wisp of a prayer surprised him.

"I'm sorry, Savannah. Gabriel has tried to teach me about God and His love for us. Sometimes I do stupid things without thinking." Shane relaxed his arms on his legs, palms up in a partial shrug. "That right there was a perfect example. If a person is going to talk to God, he should do it with respect and reverence."

Gabriel picked that moment to walk up.

"Shane, there's something I need to tell you—" He perused Shane's upturned arms. "What are you doing?"

"I was waiting for God to drop a ma for Vannah on my lap."

"I see." Gabriel shook his head, used to Shane's oddities. "As I was saying—"

A shrill scream filled the air, and a bedraggled woman fell from above, landing perfectly in Shane's relaxed arms.

"Aaaieee!" Shane jerked upright, the motion allowing the woman to settle fully onto his lap. "Wahh. . . ? How. . . ?"

Savannah screamed and scurried out of the way. Shane wanted to do the same, but remained frozen in place.

Emma and Lucy stood a few feet away and echoed Savannah's screams. They simultaneously burst into tears. Ben and Gabriel hurried over to scoop the girls up. Emma had been standoffish with the dark-skinned man earlier in the day, but now she buried her face against Ben's solid chest, her fear of the situation overtaking her fear of the now-familiar, kind man.

Gabriel stared, waiting for an explanation. "Shane?"

Shane shook his head. "Wh–wh—I don't understand."

"I do." Savannah had stopped screaming and crawled closer to Shane and the mysterious unconscious woman, seemingly over her initial shock. Her voice dropped to a reverent whisper. "You prayed for a ma for us girls, and God sent us one!"

"God sent us a ma?" Emma peeked around at the disheveled woman. Her face crumpled. "I want a clean ma like my last one. This one's all dirty and messy. I want my other ma back." She began to cry.

Lucy kept her head on Gabriel's shoulder, sucking on her thumb and watching with horrified eyes.

"You prayed for a ma for the girls, Shane? *That's* what you meant a moment ago?" Gabriel's voice was laced with disgust. "I hope you meant it from the heart because God doesn't want us taking prayer—"

"I already apologized to both God and Van, Gabe. And I sure didn't know God would answer! Not like this." Shane gently placed the woman on the soft grass and backed a safe distance away. "Not exactly anyway. I was just trying to prove a point to Savannah. Van said she wanted me to find them a ma and then settle in as the girls' pa. I said God would have to drop a ma for them on my lap."

"And He did." Savannah looked at Shane, her eyes full of wonderment. The wonderment changed to confusion, and her mouth dropped into a frown. "But I wanted a ma that could take care of us. Seems God sent us a broken-down one instead."

"He sure enough did answer that prayer, Savannah, whether Shane's words were heartfelt or not." Gabriel raised an eyebrow and sent Shane a pointed glare. He wrapped his arm around Savannah's shoulder. "God works in mysterious ways."

"My words were heartfelt," Shane muttered. He felt a certain level of satisfaction for placing the startled look on Gabriel's face.

Gabriel recovered quickly and leaned forward and peered at the woman. "She does look a bit worse for wear. Is she breathing?"

Worry crinkled Savannah's features. "She's all right, isn't she, Shane? Our new ma ain't already dead, is she?"

Shane didn't want to go near the woman. The past five minutes had taken at least a decade off his life. The whole day was something nightmares were made of—everything from finding the girls' home burned down to suddenly having six people in his care. He wanted nothing more at the moment than to hop on his mount and ride off into the sunset—alone. "I'm sure she's fine. She was breathing when I held her."

"You mean when God *dropped her on your lap*?" Gabriel inserted. "I'm telling you, Shane, God's trying to get your attention. I suggest you listen to Him."

"I'd listen to Him, too." Savannah nodded in agreement. "He sure enough did drop our ma right down, just as Shane asked Him to. She done fell straight out of the sky."

Ben had remained silent throughout the exchange. Shane looked over at him. Ben clutched Emma tight against him, looking like he'd seen a ghost.

"You okay, Ben? I'm sure she's fine, whoever she is."

"How'd she drop down from the sky like that?" Ben's words came in gasps. He slowly moved forward and deposited Emma next to Shane. "I ain't never seen nothin' like that in all my days."

"I don't figure she fell from the sky. More likely she was in the tree above us for some reason. She probably screamed because she lost her grip, and then she fainted from the fright." Shane motioned to Gabriel to come and sit with the girls. Gabriel brought Lucy and settled down between Emma and Savannah as Shane reluctantly moved forward to check on their new arrival.

The woman's face was hidden by her untidy hair. Shane gently pushed it back. She had a nasty gash on her forehead and several bruises on her face. "She's had a rough time."

Figures God would send me a misfit to mother the girls. Shane didn't deserve any better. His intentions the past few years hadn't exactly been the best when it came to a relationship with his Heavenly Father. A sense of shame flowed through him. He'd told Savannah that their ma had taught her better when it came to her words and speech. Well, their ma had taught *him* better when it came to loving the Lord.

Shane felt compelled to whisper a heartfelt prayer for the woman, his first in a long, long time. God had blessed him through the well-being of his sisters. He'd allowed Emma to pull through the same illness that took her ma away from her. He'd answered Shane's sarcastic prayer for a ma for the girls in the most surprising manner. And Shane wondered if He'd possibly answered this broken and abused woman's prayer by sending them to help her.

Lord, it's been a long time since I've talked to You, and I'm sorry. I'm sorry for drifting away in anger. Instead of turning to You in my grief the past few years, I shut You out. You've tried to get my attention through Gabe, and I've continued to shut You out. I want the peace that he has. Please forgive me and take the lead in my life as I move forward. I want You at the reins wherever I go. I give You my heart, my future, and my will. I'll even give up my—he stuttered a bit on the next few words. They came hard for him—*my cards. I'll give them up for You. Amen.*

In that moment, as he stared down at the quiet form in front of him, Shane felt a powerful tug on his heart. All these years, everything Gabriel had told him, all his preaching and teaching—the words and the verses and the parables—now wrapped around him like a comforting cloak. He felt God's presence in a very real way, a presence he'd never felt before. He knew everything would work out for the best, for all of them, this strange woman included.

"This woman"—Ben's voice cut through Shane's wonderment—"she's my mistress—from the plantation."

Shane's focus had fully been on God and the miracle the past few minutes had worked in Shane's heart. He knew he had a long way to go, but this was a good start. Shane longed to explore the revelations more fully. He glanced up at the newcomer. "I'm sorry, Ben. What did you say?"

"The woman. She be my mistress from the plantation, Miz Lydia. And from the look o' things, those wicked men who took her sure did give her a beatin'." Anger laced his words.

A shock rolled through Shane's body. He pinched himself. Surely he was dreaming. The moment couldn't get any stranger. "Did you say—Lydia?"

"Yes, suh."

Shane tilted his head for a better look. Though beaten and dirty, he could see the similarities to the bright, clean, spunky woman he'd met in town, the one who had turned his head. His heart broke a little as he stared down at her. What horrors had she been through since she'd stood on the walkway in town the previous day? He was disappointed that on the heels of his reunion with God, white-hot anger like he'd never known roiled through his soul.

I'm sorry, Lord, but if I ever get my hands on the men who did this to her, I won't be able to control myself. I'm sorry for my thoughts and anger, but I hope righteous anger is acceptable.

Later he'd discuss his conflicting feelings and confusion with Gabriel. For now he needed to tend to the broken woman that God had laid before him. After that he'd go and set things to rights with her poor excuse of a stepfather.

He flinched as her eyes flickered. After their meeting in the saloon, she'd likely come after him like a wildcat.

seven

Lydia felt her world shift and tried to open her eyes. She peered up into a circle of faces, the nearest one vaguely familiar, the others a blur. She smiled at the man who leaned over her, then sighed as she cupped his cheek. "My hero. You came for me. You're my answer to prayer."

Shock filled the man's handsome features. His blue eyes widened as his hands waved out in front of him. "Huh-uh. You've got it all wrong. I'm nobody's hero. I'm far from a hero."

Judging by his reaction, of all the words he'd expected her to utter, those hadn't been anywhere close to the ones he'd conjured in his mind.

He scowled. "And I've never been called anyone's answer to prayer. I don't think that's right."

"You're wrong," Lydia argued. She caressed his rough cheek with her thumb. "I prayed for you, and here you are. God sent you here. You are the answer to my prayer."

A young voice agreed from somewhere behind him. "She's right, Shane."

The man momentarily closed his eyes as he cupped his hand over hers, holding the palm of her hand against his face for a moment longer.

Lydia could feel her heart beating loud and strong. Her hand tingled where his strong hand touched it. She wondered if he felt the strange sensations, too. He suddenly pulled her hand away from his face and cleared his throat. "You're hurt. What hurts the most?"

She grimaced. "Everything."

"Do you feel like anything's broken?" His reassuring grip on her elbow calmed her racing heart. He stared into her eyes.

"N–no." She had a hard time focusing when he stared at her like that.

"Can you stand?"

His intense gaze made her feel weaker than she was, but she wasn't about to admit that. "I walked here. I think I'm only bruised and sore. I don't think anything's broken. Unless—"

"Unless?" His forehead creased.

"Unless I suffered a new injury after my fall from the tree." She raised her eyes to look above her and frowned. "I felt dizzy, and before I could move to a more secure position, I felt myself tipping off the branch, but I couldn't react in time to stop myself. Everything went black. How'd I—?"

"I caught you." Shane grinned. "It's a long story."

"Well, the short of it, Miz Lydie, is you be safe." Ben stepped forward, catching her by surprise, a huge grin brightening his dark features.

"Ben!" She reached up to hug him. "You're safe. I've been so worried."

She sat forward and struggled to stand. "We have to get back and save the children."

"Whoa, whoa, whoa!" Shane raised his arms and waved them in a bid for attention. "You just survived a fall from a tree and, from the looks of things, a serious beating. You aren't going anywhere for now."

Daggers flew from her eyes as she settled back on her elbows. "I'll do as I please. My siblings need me. I'll not tarry when they still reside under the roof of a madman."

"Mister Shane's right, Mistress. We be goin' back fo' the

others, but not till we know you be okay."

Lydia raised an eyebrow. "Ben, please don't ever call me 'mistress' again. I've never been your mistress, nor will I ever be. You're a free man. We're simply friends from here on out."

"Yes'm." Ben dipped his head in a submissive gesture.

Lydia sighed. Lifelong habits were hard to break. She'd work with him on that later.

She made another attempt at sitting up. Shane took her arms and assisted her to a sitting position, though she sat more by his strength than any of her own. She enjoyed the sensation. She wished she could lean against him like she had in her earlier musings.

Shane introduced her to several cute little girls and his friend Gabriel before motioning for her to relax. "We were about to eat the noonday meal when you—dropped in. It's a bit late, but we've been traveling, too. Why don't you join us? As soon as we're finished, we'll head out. We're going to our homestead, which isn't too far away. I'm afraid it'll be in poor condition after being neglected for the past few years, but a little work will set it to rights soon enough." He hesitated. "You'll be safe there."

"About that, Shane. . ." The man called Gabriel looked nervous.

Shane frowned. "You don't think she'll be safe?"

"It's not that, it's just—"

"Anything else can wait." Shane waved him off. He looked back at Lydia. "Do you think you can travel a bit farther today?"

Lydia nodded. "I'll be fine as soon as I eat. As a matter of fact, I'm fine with eating as we go."

"We'll eat here."

"But—" Lydia bristled. She didn't like to be bossed around by anyone, and she had one goal in life—to get to her brothers and sister. Her argument died on her lips. Shane had already moved away to get their food.

❧

"What happened to our brothers, Shane? I don't remember them."

Savannah sat on the far side of Lydia, flanking her on the wagon's bench. Lydia leaned against Shane's arm. The rhythm of the horses' hooves had quickly lulled her into a deep sleep.

"They left for the war right before you were born. I stayed behind to take care of Ma."

"Weren't you old enough to go?"

He nodded. "In theory, yes. There were boys younger than me who'd joined the cause, though many of them lied about their age. I'd just turned fifteen when our brothers left, but Ma needed me at home."

Savannah looked surprised. "You stayed behind to help Ma?"

"I haven't always been a rambling, no-account, Van."

"I never thought you were a no-account." She played with her skirt.

Shane glanced down at Lydia. She hadn't moved. Ben sat in the back of the wagon, entertaining the little girls with his chatter.

"What happened to our brothers?"

"Edward was killed in battle a few months before the war ended."

"I'm sorry."

Shane smiled to see this sensitive side of his sister. Edward was just as much her brother as he was his, but she didn't see it that way. He hadn't been close to his brothers by the time they'd left, but Savannah had never known them.

"Thanks."

"What happened to the other one?"

"Lucas made it through the war and returned home."

"And something happened to him, too?"

"Yes." The wagon jerked as they started to climb. The road wound upward into the tree-clad mountainside. This last little bit of the journey would take them uphill. His anticipation grew as he suddenly realized he was going home. For the first time in four years, he looked forward to seeing their old place.

"What *happened* to him, Shane?" Exasperated, Savannah kicked her feet against the front of the wagon.

Lydia shifted beside him.

"He made it through the war, tough as can be, but after he left the homestead, he took ill and died without us ever knowing it'd happened. Apparently, he'd been injured in the war, and infection weakened him and took his life."

"How did you find out?"

"His pastor friend sent us a note. He said Lucas had died but that he'd asked the Lord to be his Savior on his deathbed." Shane watched as Gabriel dropped back to ride beside them.

"You never got to say good-bye?"

"No, I was busy helping Ma with you, and then Pa came home for a bit, and next thing I knew, we had Lucy to care for. Ma was sickly after Lucy came, and then she passed away, too."

"You've lost a lot of people you love. No wonder you sent us away."

Shane tilted his head sideways and observed her. Did she really comprehend him that well? The fact that he'd lost so much, he was afraid to hold too tight to the girls in case he lost them, too? "You think I sent you away so I'd not feel hurt again if something happened to you?"

Savannah giggled. "No, I figured you sent us away because you seem to have bad luck when it comes to lovin' somebody, and you didn't want to bring that bad luck on us."

Shane reached over and tugged her black braid. "You really believe in bad luck?"

"No." She tugged her braid from his grasp. "But I sure do love teasing you." She settled back on her seat. "I think you'll do a fine job keeping us safe, just as you always have."

His heart hitched. He didn't feel like he'd done such a good job of late. "Well, it's good that you feel that way, Van, because I intend to be around for a long, long time. I'll be around so long I'll handpick your beaus and pull my shotgun on any of the boys that come around so I can send them scurrying."

Savannah raised an eyebrow. "You'll have to get past me first, 'cause any boy comes callin' on me and I'll have my shotgun out before you ever see him. I don't take kindly to any boys wantin' to court me."

"Promise?"

"Promise!"

Shane laughed out loud. "That's my girl." Now if only she'd hold to that grand promise for another twenty years or so, it'd be fine with him.

They rode in silence for a bit. Vines and overgrowth crowded the rugged road. They jarred and bumped along the ruts. The breezes carried with them the smell of spring mixed in with freshly kicked-up dust. The road had narrowed considerably from when they'd started, and Shane wondered if they'd be able to make the full trip in the wagon. Gabriel rode alongside them, a feat that wouldn't be possible if the road narrowed further.

Shane nodded ahead. "You think we can make it all the way in?"

"I don't think it narrows much more after this. I thought I'd ride ahead and look things over."

"That might be a good idea."

Gabriel spurred Twister to move ahead. The huge beast hurried to obey. The other horses seemed to make him nervous. Shane watched as they rounded a curve and disappeared from sight.

"I came in from the path and followed the road 'bout here," Ben's voice called from the back. "I seen it as I walked through the woods, and it looked to be about the same up 'head from what I saw."

"Thanks, Ben." Shane looked at the overgrowth and understood a bit more why Ben's ankles were so torn up. The shackles had done their damage, but the weeds, roots, and branches he'd walked through hadn't helped.

"Why's it getting so rugged anyways?" Savannah asked. "Don't nobody live out here no more?"

"Anybody," Shane corrected.

"Don't anybody live out this way?" Savannah tried again.

"Doesn't anybody?"

Savannah leaned around Lydia, staring at him in confusion. "That's what I asked you."

"You say it like this, 'Doesn't anybody live out here anymore?'"

Savannah carefully enunciated her next few words. "Doesn't anybody live out this way no more?"

Lydia, awakened now that the road had roughened, laughed. Shane found himself grinning along with her—until she lifted her head from his shoulder. He frowned at that and wanted to pull her back against him. With effort, he refrained.

She glanced around. "Where are we?"

"We're getting pretty close to the homestead. We haven't

been there for several years. The buildings should be intact, but I'm sure we'll have some cleaning up to do to make them habitable. We'll make quick work of it, though, don't you worry."

"I'm not worried." Her expression clouded. "Not about that anyway."

"What are you worried about?"

"My stepfather finding Ben and me. My sister and brothers being hurt while I'm away."

"We're going to get them out of there."

She nodded, but didn't look convinced. She'd pulled her hair back from her face and secured it at the nape of her neck with one of the new ribbons he'd brought for Savannah. The bruises on the soft skin of her face reinforced the reason for her concern.

"We haven't passed anyone, have we? While I was sleeping?"

"No, and we won't this far out. This road circles out from town and backs up on a private mountain. My father's family owned the mountain for as far back as anyone remembers. I suppose it belongs to the girls and me now, though I've not really given it much thought until now."

"We own a whole mountain?" Savannah bounced on the seat.

"I reckon we do."

Lydia contemplated that. "And what lies on the far side of your homestead? Does your family own whatever is there, too?"

"No. The land beside us isn't worth much. It's all trees and hills and rocks. Ma didn't talk much about that, and my pa was so seldom home, I didn't ask who owned it."

"There's a good chance it back up on yo' place, Miz Lydie," Ben piped up from the back of the wagon where he'd been telling the stories that so wonderfully entertained Emma and Lucy. "Yo' pa's land run right back to the mountain, and this here's the same mountain it backs up on. Unless I's wrong, we done circled around to the back of the plantation."

"We're heading toward the plantation?" Lydia's words came in a panicked burst.

Shane nodded. "I suppose so, but in a roundabout way. The road from town heads east, and we rode out and headed north to get to Emma, Lucy, and Savannah." They hadn't filled Lydia in on that part of their day. "Now we're heading west again. If your place backs up to the mountain, we're heading that way now. But we're talking a no-man's-land. The land between our homesteads is wild and overgrown."

"That it is," Ben muttered.

Lydia leaned forward, her knuckles going white where she clutched the bench. "We need to go back, Ben. We need to get you out of here. What if Joseph's men find you?"

"I be safe out here, Miz Lydie. I done told you I had some friends working to help me and my missus escape. They live right back here on this edge of the plantation."

Shane frowned. "I'm afraid you've got that wrong, Ben, unless we're at a different angle from where the plantation backs up to the mountain. Our place is the only homestead out here. Maria was our nearest neighbor."

"I had no idea we were so close to home!" Savannah pouted. "If Maria lived so close, why was she the last one you left us with?"

"I suppose I felt the need to keep you girls far away from the homestead, Van. I can't rightly say why, but obviously it doesn't matter anymore 'cause just around that bend we'll see home again."

eight

They rounded the bend, and Lydia leaned forward for her first glimpse of her new temporary home. She glanced sideways and raised an eyebrow at Shane. "Your homestead doesn't look nearly as bad as you presented it."

Shane reined in the horses. "This can't be right."

Savannah mimicked Lydia's movements, leaning forward and holding a few dark strands of stray hair out of her face. "Why can't it be right? Is this our house or ain't it?"

"Isn't it," Shane corrected, his brows furrowed. "It's our place, but it should be well on its way to being buried in weeds by now. We've been gone four years. When we lived here, it was a constant battle to keep the foliage from growing back and taking over the grounds."

A two-story home with covered porches wrapping around the front and both sides stood proudly in the center of a crisp clearing. Flowers circled the base of the house, circled each of the trees that stood sentry out front, and lined up in a neat row along the walkway. Spanish moss hung from the huge trees that flanked both sides of the yard. More moss-laden trees filled the land as far as the eye could see. Gray curls of smoke curled from the chimney and wafted their way on the breeze. The comforting scent of wood smoke tickled Lydia's nose and welcomed her to the spread.

In the distance, freshly planted fields stretched out along the base of the mountain.

Ben and the little girls sat quietly in the back of the wagon.

"Someone most definitely lives here, Shane." Lydia's heart fell. She'd been ready for a good night's sleep in a soft bed so they could wake up fresh and ready to figure out a way to save her sister and brothers.

"I can only think of one explanation." A muscle worked in Shane's jaw. "We have squatters."

"Bold ones at that." Lydia felt a chill race up her spine. What if the squatters were Joseph's people?

"What're squatters?" Savannah asked, her voice serious as she reached across Lydia and placed her hand on Shane's leg. Lydia wrapped a reassuring arm around the thin girl's shoulders. "Does that mean we don't have a home after all?"

"Squatters are people who try to take over someone else's home." Shane growled. He squeezed Savannah's hand. "I'm not having you lose two homes in one day, Van. The squatters are the ones who'll lose their home this time around, not us."

This was a side of Shane Lydia hadn't seen at the saloon. He'd been angry, but fair with her younger brother. Wyatt had apparently caused Shane to lose a good amount of money and shouldn't have been in the saloon in the first place. Other men would have been far harsher. He'd been kind to her younger brother despite the money lost. This irritated side of Shane was ready to take matters into his own hands no matter what the outcome. Yet he didn't show any of the raw anger Joseph always displayed. Lydia still felt safe in his care, even though he was angry.

"Where's Gabe?" Savannah glanced around, her question momentarily distracting Shane and wiping the scowl from his face.

Realization dawned on his features. "Good question, Savannah. Where *is* Gabe? Seems he was in a mighty big hurry to get over here before we did."

"And he kept trying to tell you something after you said we were coming home. He looked worried."

"Hmm, he did, didn't he? I should have paid more attention." He shrugged, once again the easygoing man she'd first met. "Maybe we don't have squatters after all. Let's find out what's going on."

Lydia touched his arm. "Maybe Ben and I should remain in the wagon until you do know who's living here."

"You'll be fine." Shane shook the reins and set the wagon in motion.

Lydia glared and pulled her shoulder away from where it touched his. She crossed her arms in front of her to further prevent contact. A moment earlier she'd enjoyed the strong security his closeness represented; now his closeness annoyed her.

He sighed. "If there'd been a problem, Gabriel would have warned us. Savannah has a point. Whoever is living here is staying with Gabriel's blessing."

"You're sure?" Lydia wasn't. Again she wished Shane wasn't so authoritative. This was the Shane from the saloon—confident and cocky.

At that moment, Gabriel and two other dark-skinned people exited the front door of the home. They stood on the porch as Shane pulled the wagon to a stop and jumped to the ground. He motioned for the others to stay put.

"Gabe?"

"I'd, um, like you to meet your caretakers, Matilda—"

"Please," inserted the dark-skinned woman. She stood regal and tall. A scarf covered most of her short gray hair. "Call me Tildy."

Shane nodded. "Tildy."

Lydia almost laughed at Shane's confused expression. She

felt safe. The couple wasn't one she'd ever seen before, and Gabriel did indeed seem to know them.

The light breeze blew a strand of hair across Lydia's face. She pushed it back and inhaled the sweet scent of jasmine. The intoxicating fragrance made her want to curl up on one of the comfortable chairs on the porch while sipping a cup of sweet tea.

Gabriel motioned toward the man. "And this is Tildy's husband, Isaac."

Strong and muscular, Isaac had the look of a man who was used to hard work. "Pleased to meet you, suh."

Again Shane nodded.

Lydia watched in fascination. These people were strangers in his home, yet Shane spoke to them with complete respect. Lydia couldn't help but compare his reaction to the way Joseph treated the people he came in contact with.

Shane worked his hat in his hand for a moment, the only sign of his inner turmoil. "Gabriel, could I speak to you in private?"

Gabriel looked around as if searching for an escape, like he'd rather do anything but speak with Shane at that moment.

With no escape in sight, he moved forward and down the porch stairs. "Um, sure."

Isaac motioned toward the house. "We'll just step inside and prepare something for you all to eat. Join us whenever you're ready." He hesitated and looked over at the wagon. "If you want help with your bags—"

"We're fine for now, thank you, Isaac," Gabriel interjected.

"If you're sure—"

Gabe nodded.

Shane and Gabe walked to the far side of the wagon.

"I have *caretakers*, Gabe? Since when?"

"Since you up and abandoned the place, Shane. This is a

good spread. I wasn't about to let you lose it. Savannah and Lucy deserve to have their home intact."

"So you let strangers move in?"

"They aren't exactly strangers." Gabriel looked out over the fields.

"Suppose you tell me who they are, then." Shane crossed his arms and stared Gabriel down.

Gabriel looked uncomfortable. "My Aunt Tildy and my Uncle Isaac."

Lydia listened with interest. Gabriel had apparently hired on staff without talking to Shane, and Shane took it in stride. Her stepfather would have injured people over such a thing. Shane's only reaction was to lean back against the wagon and fold his arms across his chest.

"You didn't think this was something I needed to know?"

"I knew you'd say no."

Lydia's eyes widened.

"So you did it anyway." Shane just sighed. "Care to fill me in on the details?"

"They needed a place to stay after leaving their former home. They worked inside the house of a wealthy couple, Isaac managed the outdoor laborers and doubled as a butler, and Tildy managed the house staff. They had wonderful skills, but once they lost their positions, they had nowhere to go. The homestead was sitting here, abandoned. I told Isaac he could live here in exchange for working the land and keeping things fixed up."

"You did, did you?" Shane scowled. "And where do you propose we all sleep now that we've arrived to find the place full of people?"

"It's hardly full of people. There's plenty of room for everyone."

"I be fine sleepin' in the cabin out back if it helps, or even in the barn," Ben piped up from the back of the wagon.

Shane turned to look at him. "The cabin?"

"Yes, suh." Ben glanced at Lydia as if for reassurance. Confused, Lydia nodded for Ben to go on.

"Tildy and Isaac be the folks who wuz aidin' Sadie and me in gettin' away from Master Joseph." He lowered his eyes. "I's sorry, Miz Lydie, but we knowed that what Master Joseph wuz doin' wasn't right. We had a right to be free. We wanted to move on. Only the master got rid of Sadie 'fore we could follow through."

"I completely understand, Ben."

"They say there be a cabin in the hills for us to stay in."

"Tildy and Isaac are running an underground railroad out here?"

Gabriel rolled his eyes. "No, Shane. You know there aren't slaves anymore. Not legally anyway. Tildy and Isaac were just offering a place for people like Ben and his wife to go when they needed to get—away. They'd remain here until they could find a place to become established."

Lydia couldn't see Shane's face, but from Gabriel's reaction and the way he took a step backward, she was glad. She reached over and took Savannah's hand in hers. Surely Shane wouldn't cause a scene with the children present, but that had never stopped her stepfather.

"Okay." Shane shook his head again and pushed away from the wagon. "And what cabin are you referring to?"

"Ben's referring to your folks' original place up in the hills, the one your ancestors built. The cabin they moved into after they married. It's up the mountain a bit."

"That old place? Is it habitable?"

"It is now. Isaac and Tildy stay there most of the time. He

said it's just as nice as this place."

Tildy exited the door and motioned them in. Shane reached up to help Lydia from the wagon. She tottered at the edge of the wagon when a shaft of pain shot through her head. She was still unsteady on her feet. Shane caught her and swept her up in his arms. Gabriel moved forward and reached for Savannah. She leaped into his open arms. Gabriel lowered her to the ground, then lifted Emma and Lucy from the back. They ran around in circles, following along at Savannah's heels.

"Can we see out back?"

"Just for a few minutes. Listen for me to call." Shane's face transformed, and a gentle smile formed on his mouth as he watched the little girls scamper off with childish enthusiasm.

"I be waitin' out here." Ben moved to settle back on his pallet.

"Nonsense." Shane tipped his head toward the house. "We all go in together."

Ben looked surprised, but he nodded in agreement.

Tears filled Lydia's eyes. Ben had never been allowed to enter their plantation home, even when his wife Sadie had been working in the kitchen. Joseph hadn't treated Ben any better than his animals. In fact, the animals were often offered better respect and care than Ben.

Gabriel started to help him down, but Isaac called out to them to wait.

"Gabriel told me who you have there. Joseph came around this mornin'. He brought his dogs along and asked if we'd seen Ben. Ben shouldn't have his scent on the ground just in case he comes around again."

Ben and Lydia exchanged glances. Shane shifted her in his arms and frowned as he contemplated Isaac's words.

"Gabe, bring the wagon as close to the porch as you can. Ben can step down from there onto the porch steps."

Gabe did as Shane said. Ben shakily mounted the stairs and walked across the porch. His ankles were swollen. They looked infected. Lydia would tend to his wounds once they were all inside—that is, if Shane ever put her down.

"I'm perfectly able to walk," she chastised. Though she guessed it wouldn't do to have her scent on the ground anymore than Ben's if Joseph and his men were snooping around.

"I saw that you were able to walk, right before you swooned and fell into my arms."

"I didn't 'swoon and fall into your arms.' I merely—"

"Merely?" He smirked. "Merely what?"

She wasn't making things better. "I had a moment of dizziness, but it's passed. I'm sure I can make my way inside on my own."

"I'd rather not take any chances." He ignored her expression and followed the others onto the cozy porch and through the door.

nine

They stepped into the home and followed Tildy down the entry hall and into a warm kitchen at the back of the house. The room looked out toward an open space that was flanked by a large barn. Lydia saw Gabriel pull the wagon around into the open space and on into the barn.

Isaac hurried out the back door and down the steps to help Gabriel with the horses.

Tildy stared at Ben's sore ankles after they'd entered the room and, with a frown, motioned him to a seat at the large rectangular table. Ben eased into the wooden chair.

Shane didn't make any move to set Lydia on her feet.

Uncomfortable with Tildy's assessing stare, Lydia said, "Shane, I think I can make it from here."

"What?" Shane pulled his attention from the clearing behind the house where the girls ran free and only then seemed to realize he still held Lydia in his arms. "Oh, I'm sorry."

He carried her to the table and settled her down beside Ben.

"Y'all look a bit worse for wear," Tildy chided. "Gabriel filled us in a bit on what you have been through."

"I'm sure we'll be fine, now that we're here." Lydia smiled. She didn't want to cause the kind woman any worry. "After a good night's sleep, we can head over to the plantation and collect my brothers and sister."

Shane had moved to stand close to her side, and now he sank down into the empty chair to her right, the opposite from where Ben rested. "You aren't going anywhere fast, Lydia. You can't run off without a plan, or you'll end up worse off than you are now. We'll all sit down together and talk this through and figure out the best way to get the children as soon as we've all had a time to rest." He sent her a pointed look. "And to recuperate."

"Now's as good a time as any to make plans." Shane's reticence to hurry forward with the rescue frustrated Lydia. If it were his little sisters that were held captive, she doubted he'd even have bothered to stop by the homestead. She told him as much.

"I'd make sure I had the proper supplies and could do the rescue right the first time, Lydie. I wouldn't run off half-cocked."

"I'm not running off 'half-cocked,'" she huffed. Her heart skipped a beat at his intimate use of her nickname. "I've had plenty of time to think things through as I walked here."

Shane leaned back in his chair. "All right, then fill us in. What's the plan?"

Lydia hesitated, not sure her plan was a good one now that she had to share it. "I wanted to get them while they're out in the fields. If we don't hurry, they'll be going in for dinner. Joseph had all of us work in the fields alongside the others."

"I'm listening." Shane looked intrigued. "He doesn't have anyone watching over them?"

His interest encouraged her to go on. "That's the only problem. The men who took me away and dumped me over the side of the road sit on their horses with shotguns strategically placed on their laps and watch over the fields as everyone works. Their presence is supposed to intimidate the hands into staying on. They're grooming my brother Nathan to help."

"And how do you propose we get around these men?"

A small trill ran through her at his use of "we," but her shoulders drooped as she answered his question. "I haven't figured that part out yet."

"See? Half-cocked. That's not the type of thing you figure out when you're charging into battle, not if you don't have to." He held up a hand to still her protest. "And in this case, you don't have to."

Tildy stood at the stove dipping up bowls of savory-smelling soup. She shook her head as they talked.

Ben joined the conversation. "I can help. I don't have no suggestions 'bout gettin' rid of the foremen, but I get respect from the other workers. They be trustin' ya if ya take me along."

"Ben, I can't ask you to take that risk," Lydia hurried to say.

"But—"

She interrupted. "I can only imagine what Joseph would do if his men catch you. It's too dangerous." She motioned to his ankles. "And you can't walk that far anyway. Not until your ankles heal."

"If y'all will wash up, you can eat," Tildy said as she placed a serving of soup in front of each of them. "And I'll have a look at that ankle, Ben, as soon as you have your fill of dinner."

She crossed the room to the door and called for the girls. As they came giggling into the room, she carried a basket of cornbread and a bowl of creamy butter over to the table.

"Gabriel and Isaac will join us in a moment." She took a seat across from Ben.

The little girls settled into the two chairs beside Tildy, and Savannah glanced at the two chairs that flanked each end.

"Just choose one, child. We don't stand on formality around here."

Savannah took the chair at the end, which placed her between Emma and Shane. Lucy stared up at Tildy with a grin. "I like it here. You have a pretty house."

The grown-ups smiled as Tildy looked at Shane. Her eyes sparkled with amusement. "This is y'alls house, little one. We just been watchin' over it for you."

Lucy tilted her cherubic blond head, her blue eyes serious. "We 'preciate that."

Everyone laughed.

Lydia watched Shane's expression change from one of concern to an expression of gentle pride as he watched the interaction. He noticed Lydia watching, and the corner of his mouth quirked up.

"She's so sweet," Lydia whispered.

"I've been worried about her," he explained quietly. "Those are the first words she's spoken since her trauma in the wood box."

"That makes it all the sweeter." Lydia said a quiet prayer of thanks for Lucy's recovery and prayed for a similar outcome for Wyatt.

Gabriel and Isaac entered the kitchen, their hands dripping with water from the outdoor pump. Tildy motioned them to a towel that hung on a hook on the wall.

"Smells mighty good in here, Aunt Tildy," Gabriel said.

Tildy motioned to the seat at the end. "Have a seat, Gabriel. We'll get another chair for Isaac." She started to stand.

"Sit yourself back down, woman." Isaac waved her back. "I can find myself a chair."

He left the room and hurried back, carrying a wooden bench.

"I wanna sit on the bench!" Emma bounced in her seat,

almost falling off in her exuberance.

"Me, too!" Lucy chimed in.

"Girls—" Shane intervened, but Isaac ignored him and lifted the small girls from their chairs.

He pushed one chair back toward the window and moved the other to the far end of the row and placed it next to his wife. The bench for the girls was slid into place, and Isaac lifted the girls onto it.

"Are we all set then?" he asked.

Both girls covered their mouths and giggled.

Isaac's smile filled his face. "I'll take that as a yes." He moved to take his seat next to Tildy.

Shane thanked him.

Isaac beamed. "We're so glad y'all are here and that we finally get to meet you."

Lydia couldn't tell if Isaac knew this had all come as a huge surprise to Shane.

Before Shane could speak, Tildy motioned toward the food. "Why don't we say a prayer over the food and get to eatin' before the soup gets cold."

She reached for Gabriel's and Isaac's hands, and the others followed suit. Lydia's hand felt small in Shane's strong grip. Her fingers tingled at his touch. The prayer ended, and she was sure Shane gave her hand a gentle squeeze. She blushed and stared into her bowl of soup. Everyone began to talk.

Lydia's headache had returned. Her throbbing temples prevented her from entering into the discussion. She closed her eyes to fight off a bout of nausea.

"Miss Lydie, you look like you're about to fall asleep in your dinner." Tildy's concerned voice carried over the others' conversation.

Lydia startled. "I'm sorry. It's been a long day, and my head is starting to rebel. I'm sure a good night's sleep will remedy things."

She could feel Shane's intense stare as he studied her. "I think it's more than that, Tildy. Lydia took a pretty good beating at the hands of Joseph and his men. She has a head injury and a cut up under her hairline."

"Oh, child, why didn't you tell me before we ate?" Tildy stood.

"Finish your meal, please," Lydia insisted. She didn't like being the center of attention. "I'm fine, just a bit tired."

"Well I'll let you eat, but as soon as you're finished, we're going to get you cleaned up and tucked into bed."

Lydia would have argued, but the proposition sounded too good to resist.

"Thanks, Tildy." Shane nodded toward Lydia. "This one needs a firm hand. She can be a bit oppositional."

"I beg your pardon!" Lydia fumed.

He grinned. "As I was saying."

The others laughed.

Gabriel smiled. "It's true you knocked the chair clean out from under him in the saloon, Miss Lydia."

Her face flamed. She could only imagine what Isaac and Tildy were thinking about her after that statement. "Just call me Lydie, Gabriel."

Gabriel turned to his aunt and uncle. "Lydia's little brother wandered into the saloon just as Shane prepared to play his winning hand." He paused and sent Shane a condescending look.

Shane rolled his eyes in response.

"The lad called out the numbers and named each face card."

"Oh my." Isaac's soft chuckle filled the moment.

Tildy raised her eyebrows as she slathered butter onto a piece of cornbread. "No offense, Mr. Shane, but serves you right for being in a saloon."

Lydia snickered. "That's pretty much what I told him."

"Shane grabbed the youngster by the collar," Gabriel continued. "Just about the time Lydia came through the door."

Tildy gasped. "Oh my. I can only imagine what you felt when you walked in on that."

"I was steaming angry."

"Tsk, tsk." The woman shook her head. "I would be, too. So you walked over and knocked him flat?"

Gabriel laughed. "Oh did she ever. She swung her leg out faster than Shane could say, 'Howdy, ma'am,' and there he was, sprawled on the floor with all the patrons of the saloon looking on. His expression was one I'd never seen before, complete and utter shock."

"It wasn't like I'd lift a hand against a woman," Shane drawled. "I could have stopped her, but I didn't want to cause a scene."

Gabriel guffawed. "Didn't want to cause a scene? What was it you did, then, if not cause a scene? Face it—you didn't have a chance to react. Lydie was too fast for you."

"I'm glad you're enjoying this, Gabe."

"Oh, I am, Shane. It's not often someone bests you. Lydia seems to catch you off-guard in a way no one else ever has."

"All right then." Shane finished his last bite of soup and changed the subject. He leaned back in his chair. "What do you say we get on with fixing Lydia and Ben up?"

Gabriel sent one last grin across the table. "Aunt Tildy will fix them up in no time. She's a natural-born healer and has medicinal herbs for just about anything you can imagine."

"That's good to hear."

Isaac looked over at Lydia. "If you think you can make it a bit longer, Tildy can take care of Ben, and then I can get him settled up at the cabin while she cares for you."

"I'm fine with that." Lydie felt better after eating the satisfying meal.

"I have some cookies for the girls to enjoy in the meantime." Tildy got up and served two cookies to each little girl. They squealed with delight.

"You're going to spoil them." Shane's smile softened his words.

Tildy didn't falter; she just returned his smile. "And I'll enjoy every minute of it." Tildy poured cups of milk for each girl, then left the room to gather her supplies.

"I'll just wait here in the chair—"

"We'll wait out front on the swing," Shane corrected. "Can you walk, or do you want me to carry you?"

"I could have walked the first time. You *insisted* on carrying me."

"Fine, but if you wobble at all, I'm sweeping you off your feet and up into my arms." He seemed hesitant to let her walk and said the words with all sincerity.

Her wayward emotions heard them a different way, and she imagined what it would be like if he'd meant the words in a romantic sense. She almost swooned at the thought. Fighting the dizzying emotions, she forced one foot in front of the other and made her way up the front hall. At the door he did the very thing he'd threatened and swept her off her feet.

"I didn't even swoon!" she cried as he pulled her close against him.

Her heart pounded against her chest as she clung to his arms in surprise. His arms were strong and muscular as he gripped her in a secure embrace and walked across the wood planks.

"Shane!" Her voice was breathless, and she was glad when he shushed her. She didn't trust her voice not to break or give away her whirling emotions.

He carried her over to the wooden seat. The chains creaked as he lowered her down into place. He settled close beside her and placed his arm across the back of the seat. "I don't want your scent on the porch, just in case Joseph brings his dogs up here." His eyes twinkled.

Lydia narrowed her own eyes and stared. Shane shrugged. Lydia had a hard time believing him when he looked so amused.

His words sank in, and she appreciated the warmth and solidity of his strong body close beside her. "What if Joseph does come? Perhaps we should move inside—"

"He won't come this close to evening. It would get dark before he ever made it home. The land between your place and ours is too rough to travel at night on a whim."

Lydia settled back and leaned her head against the high wood back of the swing. Shane moved his arm to cushion it.

"If we lived so close, why didn't we ever meet?"

"I don't know." Shane started the swing into motion with his foot. Lydia closed her eyes, the motion soothing. "I suppose that even though our land touches, the roughness of the terrain in between prevented much exploring. My brothers and I spent most of our time up on the mountain."

"And we were expected to stay close to home and help out." Her voice quieted. "I wish I were there right now. I can't help but wonder what Wyatt's been thinking. He probably thinks I abandoned him. I want to be there with him."

"I know you do." Shane cupped her shoulder and gave it a

quick squeeze before returning his hand to the back of the swing. "But would you truly want to be there, knowing your wedding to Joseph was imminent?"

She sighed. "If it meant my siblings were safe, then yes."

A shudder passed through her.

"Your body says differently." His words were soft. "I'm not happy that you were hurt, but I'm glad you aren't there anymore. I'm glad you found us. We'll find a way to get the others out. I promise."

"You didn't seem so sure about my presence when I dropped onto your lap."

"I'd had a hard day." He grinned. "I'm a loner, and I had just been saddled with three little girls, and then Ben, and then you. That's a lot of companionship for a man to take all at once."

"You were *saddled* with us all?!" Lydia tried to pull away.

Shane wrapped his arm around her shoulder and held her tight against him. "That's how it felt at the time."

"But now?"

"Now, I'm kind of liking things as they are." He thought a moment. "I know if Savannah or Lucy or Emma were in a situation similar to yours, I'd do anything in my power to get to them and to rectify the situation. I can't do anything less for you and Wyatt. I kind of like the kid, even though he did cost me a small fortune."

Lydia punched him in the arm.

ten

Dusk fell as Shane and Lydia sat in quiet contemplation. Locusts filled the night with music. The scent of jasmine lingered in the cooling air. Lydia felt much too comfortable snuggled up as she was next to Shane. She shifted and started to move away.

"Don't move." Shane cupped her shoulder.

"I don't want anyone thinking us improper."

"Improper according to whom? There's only you and I out here." Shane tightened his hold on her arm. "Besides, I own the place."

"I don't want Tildy or Gabe or Ben to think ill of us or to get the wrong impression. And we need to consider the little girls—"

"I guess I have a lot to learn about what folks consider improper. We're not doing anything untoward, Lydia. And if I let go of you in your present state, you'll likely tumble onto the porch. I doubt anyone would think that a proper action to allow from a gentleman like me. Stop worrying and let someone take care of you for a change. Relax."

Shane had a point. Lydia hadn't had an opportunity to have someone else care for her, not in a long, long time. She thought about it a moment. Not since her mother had passed away. Sadie had tried to mother them, but Joseph always intervened, trying to keep her away.

Lydia allowed her mind to drift. She wondered what it would be like to know Wyatt and the twins were tucked safely away inside Shane's house along with Emma, Lucy, and Savannah. She considered how nice it would be to spend each evening with Shane in a similar manner to this, swaying on the swing, the two of them discussing their accomplishments at the end of the day, and then planning together for the day that would follow.

The swing creaked as Shane toed it along, and Lydia closed her eyes. She savored the magical thought and wished the moment could last forever. She might not ever enjoy such a pleasant routine in her daily life, but she could certainly take pleasure in the experience while she had it. At Shane's side, she felt protected and safe.

"I'm ready for you, Miss Lydie." Tildy's cheerful voice interfered with Lydia's musings and shattered them, ruining the moment as suddenly as she stepped onto the porch. She hesitated. "Oh dear, I'm sorry. Did she fall asleep?"

"I think she might ha—" Shane started.

"No, Tildy, I'm awake," Lydia interrupted, her voice groggy. Maybe she had fallen asleep.

Shane stayed her with his hand. "Let me help you inside. Joseph's dogs, remember?"

Lydia remembered all too well.

He carried her into the foyer. "I'll go out back and check in with Isaac and Gabriel. We'll come up with a basic plan." He set her down just inside the front door.

She felt bereft. "I want in on the discussion."

He was shaking his head before she finished. "You need to let Tildy tend to that cut. You get cleaned up, and we'll fill you in on our plans come morning."

Tildy nodded her agreement and nudged Lydia toward the kitchen. Shane passed through the kitchen and exited the back door. Lydia longed to go with him.

"Go sit on that chair, and I'll be right with you." Tildy walked over to the stove. "I hope you don't mind, but I took a bit of extra time to clean the young'uns and tuck them into bed before comin' for you."

Lydia didn't mind. It allowed her more time with Shane. "I wasn't going anywhere."

"So I noticed. You and Mister Shane sure looked cozy on that swing."

"Oh—I didn't mean to act inappropria—"

Tildy shushed her. "You didn't do anything wrong, child. Seems to me you could use some pamperin'. From what Gabe told me, you've not had much in the way of leisure with that awful stepfather of yours. And with that said, it's my turn to pamper you. For a long time I've not had anyone but Isaac to fuss over, and he doesn't take very well to fussin'."

"I can imagine." Lydia sank gratefully into the chair. Everything felt woozy. "Fuss away."

"I enjoyed cleanin' up the little girls and tuckin' them into the fresh clothes Gabriel fetched for me. The poor little things were asleep before I left the room. The water from their bath was dirtier than bathwater from Isaac after he works in the fields! I had fresh water drawn for you."

"Thank you."

A warm bath sounded heavenly, even though Lydia had nothing clean to put on after. She glanced over and saw that someone had dragged a large tub into place in front of the roaring fire. Hot water steamed on the stove. Tildy dipped some and placed it into another, smaller pan and placed it on the table next to a white cloth. "We'll start with the gash on your head. Let me take a look."

Tildy's small intake of breath let Lydia know the gash wasn't a small one. "Is it bad?"

"I don't know how you've managed to stand on your feet after a knock like this. It's a miracle pure and simple that you were able to think clearly enough to get up and find help as you did."

"Thank you, Lord," Lydia mumbled.

"That's exactly right. Um-hmm. Thank the good Lord indeed. He was watchin' over you, child. Watchin' over all of you it seems. He has a plan in motion and must have had it goin' for a long time to pull you all together like this. Each one of you seems to need the other."

Lydia felt her face warm. "Oh, I don't know about that."

"Well I do. And those little girls need a family," Tildy stated as she gently cleaned the area around the wound. "I can see the beauty of His plan as clear as I can see the pretty little nose on your face."

Lydia resisted the urge to roll her eyes.

Tildy continued talking. "You all were meant to be together. That man out there is smitten by you, and I'm thinkin' you have similar feelings for him. I'm gonna enjoy sittin' back and watchin' the Lord work His miracles in both of your lives."

"Tildy, please! You're making me blush."

"Well hold on tight to that chair, honey, because now I'm about to make you yell in pain."

Even pain sounded like a good diversion from where their conversation had been heading. Lydia rethought that statement a few moments later. Tildy didn't hold back when she scrubbed the filthy wounds.

"I don't want this wound to get infected so I have to clean it well. I know it hurts."

At one point Lydia cried out, and footsteps pounded up the back steps. "Everything all right in there?"

Tildy snickered. "We're doin' just fine, Mister Shane. You go on and don't worry about this pretty lady none. She's in good hands with me."

"Lydia?"

Tildy raised her eyebrows and sent Lydia a knowing look.

The heat crept back up Lydia's cheeks. "I'm fine, Shane. Thanks for asking."

"Told you he has it bad for you," Tildy said in a quiet voice. "He's been sittin' out there on that porch just waitin' for a chance to check up on you, and you've only been out of his sight for a few minutes." She grinned. "Um-hum, he's got it bad for sure."

Lydia tried to fight off the small smile that threatened to turn into a full-fledged grin. "He probably doesn't want me to bleed all over his nice, clean kitchen."

"Oh I think the man knows I can clean the kitchen and put it back to rights whether you bleed all over or not. It was a wreck when we got here, and I got it to looking like this. I reckon I can do it again."

Though she listened hard, Lydia didn't hear the sound of Shane's boots thumping down the steps.

"He's gonna sit out there and wait until he knows you're all right." Tildy shook her head. "We gonna have to hurry and fix you up so he can get on with his plans."

With the worst of the cleaning over, Lydia was able to relax against the chair. Tildy made quick work of the other small cuts and then directed Lydia toward the bath.

"You can go now, Mister Shane."

Lydia jumped as Tildy yelled through the door.

"We're just fine in here. You can be on your way. Miss Lydia sat through my abuse to her cuts brave as can be, but now she's about to climb into a warm bath. You're free to go on out and get some work done now."

Shane's chuckle drifted through the closed door. "Thanks for the update, Tildy. I suppose I'll do just that."

Lydia buried her mortified face in her hands.

❧

Shane stalked off toward the barn. He couldn't believe he'd been so obvious sitting outside the door like that. What had gotten into him? Lydia wasn't exactly the damsel-in-distress type. She'd been a force to be reckoned with at the saloon! Granted, the head injury made her appear more vulnerable and had put her in a weakened state, but he had no doubt the ferocious woman he'd first met was waiting just below the surface.

If he gave her half a chance, she'd probably lay him flat again as soon as she recuperated. And he'd enjoy every moment. That thought made his mind go in all the wrong directions. He pushed away the image of him pulling her down along with him and forced his wayward thoughts in another, more proper direction.

Truth of it was, Lydia had gotten under his skin—something no other woman had ever been able to accomplish. He'd always been more of a love-'em-and-leave-'em type of a man, but Lydia lingered in his thoughts, and she'd even invaded his dreams the previous night at the hotel.

The woman he'd met in town seemed reserved and aloof. This version of Lydia was warm and in need of his protection. He wondered which was the real Lydia. Perhaps she was a bit of both. He moseyed in the general direction of the barn, walking slowly to savor the moment of aloneness.

Twister, Pal, and Chester waited in the corral beside the barn. Shane could hear their grunts and whickers as he passed by.

He walked over to the recently reinforced fence and leaned

against it to reach his hand toward Pal. Pal walked over and let Shane rub his nose. The large moon reflected off his brown eyes.

"How ya doin', Pal? Does it feel good to be home? No livery, no hitchin' post—just you and your buddies relaxing in the fresh evening air."

Pal tossed his head and snorted.

"I'm kind of enjoying it, too, buddy. Much more than I expected."

Of course it helped to come home to a warm, inviting house instead of the mess of a place he'd envisioned. This life beckoned to him, begged him to step back in. He found himself wondering why he'd ever left in the first place.

He'd felt lost after his father and brothers left. That part he knew. He'd wanted to look around and see if he found a better fit for himself outside the homestead. He'd given in to wanderlust, wanting to know if he was like his father, only to discover he didn't find peace on the trail. Yet he'd had it here at the house. The closer they had come, the closer he'd felt to God. Had Shane chased all over the state for something that was here all along?

He knew he wasn't his father. He wasn't his brothers. He actually liked working the earth and seeing the fruits of his labor pay off when fresh green plants pushed their way through the soil and reached toward the warm sun. Why had it taken four long years for that realization to dawn?

He found himself looking back toward the house.

Maybe he'd needed a gentle prod. A few years earlier, he hadn't felt fit to raise Savannah, let alone a baby. He was exhausted after caring for his mother, the homestead, and the two little girls. He'd made the decision to place his sisters in a home where they could get a mother's love. Instead,

Savannah had done her best to thwart his every plan, only wanting to come home. He owed them both an apology.

He'd been selfish to abandon them and take away the only security they had left. He'd only thought of himself when he'd hit the trail. And in the mix, he'd almost lost the girls, too. The only family he had left.

Again, he realized what a miracle it was that they'd survived the fire and were back in his care. He wouldn't blow it again. No matter what decision he made for the future, he'd make sure the plan worked with the three little girls by his side.

He figured he'd dawdled long enough and walked into the barn. The sweet scent of fresh hay tickled his nose. He drew it in, savoring the familiar fragrance.

Gabriel and Isaac were hard at work inside the large structure. Shane didn't have the heart to make them sit down to a meeting this late when they were all tired. The discussion and planning could wait until tomorrow. That way Lydia could join in, too.

"'Bout time you decided to join us," Gabriel teased. "I thought you were going to sit on the porch all night like a little lovesick puppy." He paused before adding, "A lovesick puppy who has been relegated to the back yard for the night."

Shane threw a handful of hay at Gabriel, and Gabriel ducked.

Shane had never seen this side of his friend. The Gabriel he knew tagged along on Shane's heels, going wherever Shane chose to go, nagging and preaching at him along the way. This Gabriel wore his sleeves rolled high on his elbows and was filthy dirty and apparently enjoyed every moment of it. He'd regained his sense of humor.

"Hard work seems to agree with you, Gabe."

Gabe and Isaac were cleaning out the unused stalls and preparing them for the horses.

"Seems I remember you being a lot happier when you were working the land, too. I can't believe it's taken us four years to get back here."

"I can't either."

Gabriel stared at him with wide eyes. "You're actually thinking of staying?"

"I think I am." Shane smiled. "I gave up cards in an offer to God for Savannah and Lucy's safety. God gave me my answer, with Emma thrown in as a bonus."

"You have a fever or something, Shane?" Gabriel looked over at Isaac who wore a grin on his face while still shoveling hay. "I can't believe you just said an extra child to care for is a bonus when you haven't even wanted to care for your sisters."

Shane flinched. "I don't have a fever, and I mean it, Gabe. God got my attention at the cabin, and I think now He's calling me home."

"G–God?" Gabe's dark face paled a shade. "Ca–calling you home?"

Shane laughed. "Not in that way, Gabriel. Calling me back to the homestead. Calling me home to stay here."

"Whew." Gabe's eyes lit up with hope, and he wiped his forehead with his arm. "I thought for a minute there I was going to be raising three orphaned girls on my own."

Isaac called from the next stall. "You know Tildy and I would have helped, Gabe."

"I appreciate that, Uncle Isaac." Gabe leaned on his shovel and looked at Shane.

"Sorry, guys, I plan to stay around and see to that job myself."

Isaac leaned against the top of the stall and looked Shane

over. "You know, it never hurts to have a few extra hands wieldin' shotguns when you're raisin' pretty little fillies like those three in the house."

Gabriel chortled.

Shane threw back his head and joined in. "Isn't that the truth! I'll surely take you up on that offer. I'd be mighty obliged, Isaac, if you'd stay and continue with what you've been doing here."

"I was hopin' you'd say that." Isaac beamed. "I do enjoy working this place. The three of us workin' together will surely make it better."

eleven

Lydia woke the next morning to a brilliant beam of sunlight shining in her face from across the room. She glanced around at the unfamiliar space and tried to gather her bearings. White curtains were pulled across the windows, but they didn't do much to prevent the sun's glare at this late morning hour. A small table to the left of her bed held a ceramic pitcher of water, a bowl, and a crisp white towel.

The small dresser that flanked the window opposite the bed remained empty. Lydia didn't have any clothing to fill it, nothing to place in the drawers. She smoothed her hand down the soft gown Tildy had loaned her and gingerly moved to a sitting position, relieved to find that her head ached far less than it had on the previous day.

Lydia walked to the window and threw back the curtains. The sunny day lifted her spirits and made her smile. She'd slept later than she'd intended, but after the previous night of very little sleep and the hard morning of walking, she'd enjoyed the cozy warmth of the soft bed.

She turned to survey the room, wondering where Tildy had put her dress. A splash of color near the door drew her attention. A delicate pink dress with a tiny floral design was draped carefully over a nearby chair that sat between the bed and the door. She moved closer to look at it. The dress hadn't been there the night before when she'd gone to bed. Tildy must have brought it in after Lydia had fallen asleep.

The fabric looked crisp and new. Lydia knew Tildy couldn't

have whipped it up while Lydia had slept. She'd ask her new friend where the dress had come from when she next saw her. She slipped it over her head and, though it was a bit loose on the sides, it skirted the floor perfectly.

She sat to put on her freshly cleaned boots before walking over to the small vanity. A brush and a few hair accessories lay centered on top. She drew the brush through her hair, pulled her hair back, and fastened it at the nape of her neck. She quickly splashed water on her face and dried it with the waiting towel. It was so strange to find everything at the ready and not to have staged items there the night before. She was used to doing for herself. With a smile, she headed out the door.

She found Tildy hard at work in the kitchen. A lone plate and a set of silverware rested on the table in front of the farthest seat.

Tildy motioned her over to the chair. "Sit down and I'll serve your breakfast in a moment."

"Nonsense." Lydia joined her at the stove. "I can make my own breakfast. Just show me where everything is, and tell me what to make."

"You tryin' to take my job away from me?" Tildy waved a spatula in her face. "You'll have your hands full in the coming days, so take a load off your feet while you can."

"My hands full?" Lydia asked in confusion. "With what?"

"Well, you plan to gather up your siblings and get them out of your stepfather's clutches, don't you?"

"I do." Lydia hadn't given much thought to where they'd go after she collected them. The thought of bringing them back here put a lift in Lydia's spirits. Her new friend was talking as if the event would occur in the very near future! Lydia surely hoped so.

"And if you're stayin' here, you'll also have your hands full keepin' up with Emma, Lucy, and Savannah."

"I will, won't I?" Lydia loved the thought of staying and taking care of the three darling girls. But she knew Tildy was up to the task and would enjoy every minute of mothering them after her comment the night before. "You don't want to raise them?"

"I'm not goin' anywhere. But you're the one who'll be in charge if you stay."

"No one's asked me to stay." Her spirits plummeted. "Shane has only agreed to help me free Wyatt, Natalie, and Nathan. Nothing's been said about what will happen after."

"I've only just met Shane, but I've known Gabriel his whole life. I can promise you those two aren't going to put you out on your own. You'll be an asset to them if they decide to stay on, and based on what Isaac told me last night, they're plannin' to stay on."

"What a lovely thought." Lydia wandered over to the table and settled into her seat. She stared out the window and saw the men working near the barn. The little girls played nearby in the shade under a tree. She smiled. "You placed my table setting where I could best see the view. Thank you."

Tildy smiled and continued cracking eggs into a skillet. Bacon sizzled in the same large pan. The aroma set Lydia's mouth to watering. She busied herself watching Shane work. He'd donned work clothes and wore his sleeves rolled high above his elbows, much like Gabriel and Isaac. The three men appeared to work well together.

"Shane said for me to send you out to him as soon as you're finished eating." Tildy carried the frying pan over and slipped the bacon and eggs on Lydia's plate.

Lydia started to stand. "I'll go now. I can eat later. I don't want to keep Shane waiting."

"You'll do nothing of the sort." Tildy patted her shoulder. "He also said to let you sleep as long as you needed. He's in no hurry."

"I don't want him to think I'm a pampered princess. I want to do my part."

Tildy snorted. "No one thinks you're anything near a pampered princess."

"I can carry my weight and that of my siblings."

"No one doubts that, Miss Lydie. But you suffered a severe blow to the head and a very traumatic experience. We want you to heal. You won't do anyone any good if you collapse from exhaustion."

Lydia's forehead furrowed into a worried frown. "You're sure?"

Tildy sank into the chair beside her. "Positive. We talked over breakfast. Shane said you're the strongest woman he's ever met. The most stubborn, too. He wants you to rest now because he knows you won't in the future."

"He called me stubborn?" Lydia started to stand. She'd show him stubborn.

"And strong." Tildy laughed, pressing her back into her seat. "Stubborn isn't exactly an insult. It shows you have stamina and perseverance. Something every woman needs here in the foothills of the Georgia mountains."

Lydia picked up her fork and moved her eggs around on her plate. "You have to admit, 'stubborn' isn't the most romantic description he could make when speaking of me."

"Ah, you want him to speak romantic words about you?" Tildy's face lit up. "I can tell you that man isn't gonna say romantic words about you around Isaac, the girls, or me. He'll save his sweet nothin's to say to you in private."

"Tildy!" Lydia rested her elbow on the table and dropped her forehead to the palm of her hand. "It isn't like that with us."

"Maybe it isn't yet, but that day is fast a'comin'. I see it in his eyes. In your eyes, too, if truth be known."

"If so, I can do without that truth being known." Lydia laughed. "Shane whispering romantic words to me? It isn't going to happen." Though she found herself wishing it would.

"Too late for that, dearie. Your feelin's are written all over your face, plain as day."

"What feelings are written on Lydia's face?"

Lydia jumped. Shane stood in the doorway, hat in hands. His laughing blue eyes appraised her as he leaned against the doorframe. The way he grinned, Lydia figured he knew exactly what Tildy had said.

"We didn't hear you coming."

"I kind of gathered that by the startled look on your face."

Lydia forced herself to look away from his beautiful eyes and instead lowered her own and studied the way his dark hair curled against his collar. He looked larger than he had before, lounging like he was in the doorway. His broad shoulders were relaxed, his left leg crossed casually over his right ankle. He tossed his hat on a nearby hook and folded his arms. He looked as if he had all the time in the world to stand and stare at her. She continued to push her food around the plate.

"You gonna eat that food, or are you gonna just sit there and torture it?" he asked with a soft laugh.

"I've lost my appetite."

"Nonsense." He pulled out the chair at the far end of the table from her, as if moving closer would put him in harm's way. He seemed to prefer having the table between them. He gripped it with both hands.

Tildy discreetly slipped out the door that led to the hall. The coward.

"You look much better today. Does the dress suit you?"

"It does." Lydia reached down to finger the soft fabric. "You brought it for me?"

"I gave it to Tildy. She brought it into your room. It was my mother's. I hope you don't mind."

"No, it's beautiful. Thank you."

"I have several others if you'll have them. Tildy washed them and placed them in a trunk in the loft of the barn. I'll take you up later to look if you'd like."

I'd like. Lydia shivered at the thought of being alone with him in the loft. Going through a trunk of clothes with him. The experience would feel intimate.

A thought occurred to her. "Maybe you should save the dresses for Savannah. She'll be wearing them before you know it, and she might want the memory of her mother."

"I can buy her new clothes." He frowned. "Unless you'd rather I get you new ones? Not now of course, but when this is all over—when we get to town."

"You have no obligation to buy me new clothes." She couldn't meet his eyes. This whole conversation felt so strange. "If we can get back to the plantation, I'll have access to my own clothes." She glanced up at him. His intense stare made it hard for Lydia to breathe.

Shane's frown deepened. "Is that your plan? To return to the plantation and go on as if nothing happened?" He sounded angry. "You think your stepfather will welcome you back with open arms?"

His harsh tone caught her off-guard, and angry tears formed in her eyes. She dropped her gaze to hide them. "I don't expect him to welcome me at all, and I surely don't intend to live there with him." What must he think of her if he'd expect such a thing?

She dropped her fork onto her plate and dropped her hands to hug around her waist. She clutched a handful of fabric in each fist. Could Shane possibly think any less of her? Tildy was way off when it came to Shane engaging in thoughts of romance. He apparently didn't think much of her at all if he thought she'd choose to go back to that life and future.

Disappointment flooded through her. "I hadn't heard your plan yet, Shane. I merely meant I could gather my things when I gathered my siblings. I didn't see any reason why you'd be obligated to clothe me. I'm not your responsibility."

Despite her attempt to hide the angry tears, her voice cracked with emotion. "I'd appreciate your help, but as soon as I have the kids safely in my care, I'll move out of your life." She'd been way off in her daydreams. And apparently making a home here had been just that—a dream. Shane lumped her in with all the others he'd become responsible for. He only saw her as a needy orphan like Emma. Someone to provide for.

Shane was out of his chair and by her side in an instant. He knelt down on one knee and rested his elbow on the edge of the table. "I'm sorry, Lydie. I didn't mean to make you cry."

He pushed a strand of hair away from her face with his free hand. She longed for him to cup her cheek and kiss her tears away. The ridiculous thought angered her further. She'd barely known him a day, and he was toying with her emotions. And she was feeding into all the silliness. She never acted like this. Maybe her head injury wasn't as healed as she'd thought.

She glared at him. "I'm not crying." She swiped at a tear and dropped her arm back down to hug her waist. She leaned against the back of the chair to gain distance. His closeness and warm breath on her face did funny things to her stomach. "How could you even think I'd go back to him?

To Joseph. He left me for dead. He told his men to do what they wanted with me."

"You said they didn't hurt you." Shane grasped her arm, his grip gentle. Nothing in him resembled the roughness of Joseph's men.

"They didn't. Not that way." Her voice broke. "But Joseph gave them permission. How could you think so little of me that you'd think I'd go back to—to—that or to what he expects of me?"

"I don't know. But you turned down my offer for clothes and mentioned what you had at the plantation. It sounded like—" He sighed. "Will you accept my apology? I'm not good in situations like this. I'm sorry."

Lydia stared up at him through tear-filled eyes. "Situations like this?"

"That romantic talk you were discussin' with Tildy. The kind of stuff you're expectin' from me. I'm much better at this type of thing—makin' a woman steamin' mad at me."

"I don't expect romantic talk from you!" Mortified that she wanted just that, Lydia punched him in the arm. Denying the very thing she wanted the most felt much better than admitting it to him. Her voice rose as she sputtered, "I wasn't talking about us—about you—about—"

His lips were inches from hers, and she forgot what she wanted to say. "About—um—" His eyes were such a deep, intense blue. They reflected his thoughts, and right now they were searching her eyes with a pleading apology. What was it she'd been trying to say?

She didn't know how to respond to his unspoken question. *Forgive me?* He moved closer, brushing her lips with his own. Her thoughts were a muddled mess. She closed her eyes.

Shane's lips returned to close over hers, making her forget

about finding her forgotten words.

He moved a breath away. "Are you going to stop yelling now?"

"I wasn't yelling." She didn't recognize the breathless voice that answered him. She opened her eyes. Surely the voice wasn't hers. She sounded so—addled.

He brushed her lips again, addling her further. "Are you finished denying everything that's true?"

"I'm not denying—argh!"

This time Shane framed her face with his hands and pulled her tight against him. He kissed all sense out of her—that is, if she had any to begin with. And at this point, she wasn't really sure.

She swooned, grasping Shane's upper arms with her hands. She opened her eyes to see Shane staring at her in consternation.

"You surely are the most frustrating woman I've ever met. Definitely the most frustrating in the state of Georgia." He jumped fluidly to his feet, walked to the door, snatched his hat off the hook, and sent her one last look. His expression bordered on terror as he turned and stalked out the door.

Lydia looked up to see Tildy standing in the doorway fanning her face with her hands.

"Oh, honey, if that wasn't romantic, I don't know what is."

"You were *watching*?" Lydia squeaked.

"Not by choice. I heard his chair scrape back, and I thought he'd left." She fanned her face again. "I was wrong."

"Obviously. Well, maybe you can tell me what that was all about?" Lydia watched through the window as he made his way to the barn. "He's angry at me."

"Oh no. Ain't no way he's angry after that passionate of a kiss, Miss Lydie. You need to learn the difference between angry and smitten."

"I don't understand. If he's smitten, why'd he get up and stomp out of here like that?"

"He doesn't understand his emotions. Isaac acted the same way. Got all fired up and stomped around till he finally demanded I marry him."

Lydia giggled, resting her fingertips on her tingling lips. "Just like that?"

"Pretty much." Tildy rolled her eyes. "He's lucky I ever said yes, but he made up for it later. He's been a wonderful husband ever since. Some men just don't understand all the emotions that come with attraction and love."

"Love? Whoa, Tildy, slow down. We only met two days ago. We barely know each other."

"Sometimes love doesn't wait for the emotions to catch up. Y'all have it about as bad as I've ever seen it."

"As bad as you've seen what?"

"Love."

Lydia gave up trying to eat breakfast and stood.

"Where are you going?"

She looked toward the barn. "I suppose I should go out there and find out what plans the men came up with." She wiped her damp, shaky palms on the skirt of her dress.

Tildy's laugh made Lydia jump. "You look like you're walking out to face a firing squad instead of three gentle-hearted men."

"Did you *see* what just happened between Shane and me?" She waved a hand in front of her, pointing toward the barn and then back at herself. Her heart pounded at the memory, and she glanced down to see if the front of her dress moved with the rhythm. It didn't. "That can't happen again."

"Oh honey, it isn't a matter of it not happenin' again. It's just a matter of when."

twelve

Shane heard a noise and looked out through the open barn doors. He watched as Lydia exited the house and headed his way. From the expression on her face, she meant business. He wished for an easy escape but instead looked around for something to busy his hands.

Gabriel entered the side door from the corral, glanced out front, saw Lydia coming with her storm-filled expression, and headed right back out the same door.

Little girl squeals erupted from the large shade tree, and Lydia stopped in her tracks. She put a hand up to her forehead to shade her eyes, and her lips formed into a soft smile. She called out to the girls. "What are y'all up to?"

The transformation from irritated southern belle to doting female was instantaneous. The little girls obviously adored her, and according to Lydia's reaction, the feeling was mutual. The realization caused a hitch in Shane's breathing.

Savannah threw her arms around Lydia. "We're having a tea party. We found some of my old toys. Miss Tildy made us some cookies and lemonade, and later we're going to help her make more cookies!"

"Sounds wonderful." Lydia placed a hand against her heart and feigned shock. "But a tea party at this early hour? And just before we gather for lunch? Whatever was Tildy thinking?"

The younger two girls caught up with Savannah, giggling. They each took one of Lydia's hands and began tugging her arm. "C'mon. C'mon! You're just in time to fix our hair and read us a story."

"A story, huh?" Lydia looked over at the barn, and Shane backed into the shadows. "Well, I suppose I have time to join you for that. I can't resist a good story."

"You'll hafta read it to us 'cause none of us can read." Savannah sounded wistful.

It was all Shane's fault. He hadn't paid enough attention to Savannah's schooling. The years had passed so quickly! He'd make her schooling his number-one concern after he helped Lydia free her siblings.

Shane moved forward and peeked around the barn door just as Lydia sank down onto the blanket. The three girls crowded around—Savannah and Emma on either side and Lucy standing behind, her arms wrapped around Lydia's neck as she peered over her shoulder.

Lydia started reading, and the girls quietly listened. As soon as the story ended, Lydia glanced over at Savannah. Her words carried clearly. "I've been working with my younger brother, Wyatt, and he's learning to read. I can work with you, too, Savannah, if we come back here after. . ." Her voice drifted off.

"After what, Miss Lydie?" Savannah tilted her head in anticipation. Her eyes had brightened at the prospect of learning to read.

Lydia's shoulders lifted and drooped with a sigh. "We need to get my little brother and bring him back here. Shane's supposed to help me."

"Is your brother in trouble?"

"I hope not. I pray for his safety and well-being every day. I have another brother and sister I pray for, too. They're both seventeen. I'm sure they're watching out for Wyatt."

"We can pray for them right now if you want to."

Lydia's face lit up. "Thank you, Savannah!"

They bowed their heads, and Shane found himself doing the same. He said a quick prayer for the kids' safety and that they'd be able to get them off the plantation without too much trouble. He returned his gaze to the foursome under the tree. They looked so serene sitting in the magnolia's shade. The blue sky made a beautiful backdrop to the tree's green leaves. Fresh green grass covered the ground around the blanket. The pastel hues of the girls' dresses added splashes of color to the scene.

Lydia busied herself with fixing the girls' hair into fancy twists and braids.

Shane watched as Savannah gave Lydia a spontaneous hug and then placed a hand on Lydia's arm. "You don't have to worry about Wyatt and the others, Miss Lydie. Shane will get your brother back. He'll get your other brother and sister back, too, if you want him to. Shane can do anything in the world. He's strong and smart and fixes everything."

Lydia smiled. "He does, does he?" She glanced over at the barn.

Shane stepped back again.

"Yes." He could barely hear Savannah's quiet statement. He leaned around for a better view and so he could hear better. "I tend to get in a lot of trouble. Shane always comes when I need him. He always fixes things and makes them right."

"He loves you very much." Lydia hugged her and then stood, dusting off her skirt. "Each and every one of you."

"Even me?" Emma asked softly.

Lydia squatted and took Emma's hand. "Of course he loves you. I love you, too. You're a wonderful little girl and a perfect sister for Lucy and Savannah."

Emma beamed. "And you're a wonderful mama for all three of us."

Shane cringed as Lucy and Savannah nodded in exuberant agreement.

Lydia's only response was a laugh. "You girls better get back to the tea party before the ants invite themselves to your cookies." Her expression turned apprehensive. "I suppose I should go talk to Shane about fixing my situation." She started toward the barn.

"He'll fix it, you'll see," Savannah called after her.

Shane's young sister had total faith in his ability. He sure hoped he measured up.

He hurried to a dark corner of the barn, snatched up a tangled harness, and laid low. He prayed Lydia would peek in and go back into the house. He wasn't ready to explain the kiss. He didn't understand the kiss. But he knew she wanted to talk about the plan.

He needed a chance to talk to Gabriel and Isaac before talking to her about a plan. He hadn't come up with one and didn't know what to tell her. Her kisses had muddled his mind. He turned his back and fought harder with the tangled leather harness strap—the strap that had only tangled in the first place because earlier, after kissing Lydia so thoroughly, he couldn't get his thoughts away from her or force his concentration to cooperate.

And here she walked around the yard all composed and sensible, reading stories to the girls and fixing their hair as if nothing had ever happened.

"You never did get around to telling me about the plan."

He jumped when her voice sounded right behind him. So much for hoping she'd go back to the house.

Shane stilled his hands but kept his back toward her. "That's because we were too busy—" He paused. What was he going to say? *We were too busy kissing to talk about much of anything at all?*

He abruptly changed direction. "We—Gabriel, Isaac, and

I—were too busy last night to discuss today's plans. We had to prepare the stalls for the horses."

"Oh."

Shane tried to ignore the disappointment in Lydia's voice. She wanted a plan, and she wanted her brothers and sister safely away from Joseph. He couldn't blame her. He'd always hurried to Savannah and Lucy's side as soon as a summons would come.

"We'll get to it today. I promise. I plan to ride over and look the situation over this afternoon."

"Really?"

He turned to her with a frown. "You sound surprised. I've already told you I'd help."

"I know, but that was before—well—you know. Before what happened in the kitchen."

"We kissed. Why would anything change just because of that?" He tried not to scowl.

"The way you stomped out of there, I figured I'd done something wrong. I didn't ask to be kissed, but you seemed to regret it the moment you moved away."

She thought she'd done something wrong? The only thing he regretted was that he couldn't stay and kiss her again. But he couldn't tell her that.

He told her the opposite. "The kiss was a mistake. It can't happen again." He didn't want to hurt her, but they'd only just met, and he had a lot on his mind. He couldn't be slowed down by a budding romance. Now to convince his heart of that fact.

"There was more than one kiss, actually. Plural. Kisses. But I fully agree. No more kissing. That was most definitely a mistake."

She agreed way too fast. She actually sounded relieved. The thought grated on Shane's nerves.

Now he scowled. "You agree?"

Why did it matter to him that she so easily brushed off his kisses? So what if the most wonderful kisses of his life were being diminished to a silly mistake? After all, he was the one who used the stupid term *mistake*. At least now she wouldn't be making demands of him.

"Of course I agree." She moved closer.

He couldn't help but notice the way her skirt swayed daintily with each step. The sun shone through the slats of the barn and highlighted her blond hair. Her eyes sparkled as she neared.

"We've been through a lot together in the short time since we've met, Shane. It's only natural that we'd turn to each other for comfort in a weak moment."

"You found our kisses to be *comforting*?"

That didn't sit well with him at all. His entire world had been turned upside down by their kisses in a way he'd never experienced before. He'd been so muddled that he'd completely tangled the harness he was supposed to be fixing. *Comforting* was the last word he'd use to describe their kisses.

"Yes, I found the kisses to be comforting." Lydia laughed and lifted her arms in a shrug, confusion lurking in her green eyes. "What else would the kisses mean if not comfort? We barely know each other."

"You have a good point." Shane stalked across the barn. He needed to get away from her before he took her in his arms and kissed her until she admitted his kisses were much more than a means of *comfort*.

She remained where he'd left her. "About our plans—"

He had no reason to be on the far side of the barn. He fussed with a stall door before walking back to her. "*We* have no plans."

"Not true." She grinned. "We just made plans not to kiss."

She had a point, though he was trying to get his mind off kissing her. "We have no plans beyond that. I said *I'd* ride out and survey the situation at Joseph's place. You'll remain here with the girls."

"What about Ben? You'll take him along, won't you?"

He was shaking his head before she even finished. "No. I can't risk putting him in danger. He's safe at the cabin. I want to leave him there."

"Then you need to take Gabe or Isaac. I don't want you to go alone."

Maybe she cared after all.

They heard a scuffling sound in the yard. Several dogs barked in the distance.

A look of terror washed over Lydia's face.

"Joseph's dogs. Hunting dogs." Lydia enunciated each word as she looked up at Shane.

He hated the fear that lurked in her eyes. The fear this Joseph had put there.

"I walked here from the house. I left a scent for the dogs to follow. I wasn't thinking—"

Panic washed over Shane. He didn't have his gun. He had no way to defend Lydia. He'd let himself get distracted by her, and he'd let down his guard. "You'll be okay. Let me think."

The dogs were closer. Isaac and Gabriel ran from the corral and quickly herded the little girls into the safety of the house. Shane didn't have the privilege of doing the same with Lydia.

"I have an idea. Trust me." He hurried forward and swept her off her feet. He held her close as he carried her toward the ladder that led to the loft. He couldn't resist giving her the slightest of kisses. Lydia resisted, pushing hard against him.

"Put me down." Her words were angry. "You said this couldn't happen again, that kissing me was a mistake, and then you choose a time like this to sweep me up in your arms? Joseph wanted me dead. If he finds out I'm alive—" Her words were lost in a sob.

"Hush, woman. I said I have a plan." As he said it, he lifted her to the highest rung of the ladder he could reach. "I've lifted you as high as I can. Grab the ladder and get to the far back corner of the loft and stay quiet."

Lydia nodded. She hurried to do as he'd asked. She secured her boots on the rung, grasped the side of the ladder, and scurried out of sight.

thirteen

Lydia held her skirts high so she wouldn't trip and quietly moved to a better vantage point. She peered through a knot in the wood and saw Joseph and his men enter the clearing behind the house. Her heart began to pound. Isaac walked out to greet him, his demeanor casual. There was nothing casual about the rifle clutched in his hand and held at the ready. The dogs were going wild, running in circles and sniffing the ground.

"What can I do for you gentlemen?" Isaac called out, sounding like the perfect neighbor, not a hint of nerves apparent in his voice. Lydia was impressed.

Joseph had a hard time keeping his focus on Isaac. He frowned and watched as the dogs ran in frantic circles toward the barn. He studied the barn, and Lydia felt like he could see straight through it and see her cowering in the loft. Her heart pounded harder in her chest. Though Joseph watched the dogs, he made no move to follow. He returned his attention to Isaac.

"I know I've come around before, but I thought maybe I'd come back and explain a bit more about my situation."

Isaac leaned casually against the porch rail, but his grip on his rifle didn't waver. Lydia had a feeling he was completely confident and wouldn't hesitate to use the weapon in his hand. "Sure. I'm here to listen. What can I do for you?"

"Well, a couple of nights ago one of my sla—I mean, one of my workers took off with my oldest daughter."

"I'm sorry to hear that. It had to be upsetting."

"It was, in more ways than one. I've been nothing but good to Ben, and it hurts to have him turn on me like that."

He played up his hurt, shaking his head in disappointment. Lydia's stomach churned. How convenient for him. He was pinning her disappearance on Ben! If Lydia turned up dead, Ben would be tried and hanged for her murder. Joseph and his men would walk away, free of any wrongdoing. She wanted to surprise them by bursting out of the barn. She wanted to see the look on Joseph's cocky face.

"Stay put, Lydia. Let me take care of this." Shane's quiet voice carried up from below.

How'd he know what she'd been thinking?

"As you can imagine, I love my girl. I don't want to see her to come to harm," continued Joseph.

"He's lying through his teeth!" she called down to Shane in a loud whisper.

"I know he is, but we don't want an altercation right now. Not here. Ben's safely tucked away at the cabin. We'll take care of him. We need to do this right."

The dogs circled closer.

"They've picked up my scent."

"Stay put and trust me."

"I am. I do."

Joseph resumed speaking. "I don't suppose you've seen the murderous fool around here—or have you?"

"Can't say that I have. Ain't been no murderin' fools out this way that I've noticed."

"I can think of at least one," Lydia hissed.

"Lydia. Quiet!"

"Sorry."

Joseph watched the dogs circle the yard. They were waiting

for Joseph to give them permission to move on.

"The dogs seem to think otherwise. They seem to have picked up a scent."

Shane stepped into the clearing. "You think so? You're calling these people liars? From what I've seen, they haven't been anything but neighborly to you."

Joseph spun on his heels and raised his rifle. He stared at Shane for a moment. "Who are you? Are these people your workers?"

"Actually, the opposite is true. I showed up yesterday, and Isaac put me to work."

Disgust and disrespect filled Joseph's face. He'd never understand or respect a white man who worked for ex-slaves. Lydia wanted to hug Shane.

Joseph turned his back on Isaac, dismissing him, and faced Shane. "Mind if I have a look around? The dogs never make a mistake when they smell a familiar scent. Either Ben or Lydia is hiding in your barn."

Shane shrugged. "I don't mind you looking around, but that decision is up to my boss." He nodded his head toward Isaac.

Isaac played along. "Fine by me. Let me know what you find."

Lydia's heart pounded. Were Shane and Isaac going to hand her over just like that?

Joseph gave the command for the dogs to move forward, and they headed full-speed for the barn. Joseph hurried to follow them. They circled around inside and made their way back out to Shane. They sniffed and circled again. After several passes, they focused on Shane and howled their find.

"Seems to me they've found what they were looking for." Shane laughed. "Which do I resemble most, your worker or your daughter?"

Joseph glared. "I don't understand. They've never been wrong before. Get over here, you stupid dogs."

The dogs ran to him, and he swiped at them with the butt of his rifle. The dogs skirted away from him and headed for home.

Joseph lifted his rifle and pointed it at Shane. "I don't know what you have going on here, but I'll be back again soon."

Shane didn't say a word.

"Drop the rifle." Isaac's words were loud and commanding. He stood at the ready with his own rifle pointed directly at Joseph. "You aren't welcome back here in your present state. If you do come back, it better be in a neighborly fashion and without the dogs and weapon. I don't take kindly to people showin' up and pointin' a gun at my friends."

Joseph lowered his weapon, but he didn't acknowledge Isaac's command.

He motioned for his men to leave and followed them from the yard. He stopped and sent one hostile glare back that encompassed both men. Isaac waited until Joseph was well on his way before walking back inside.

Lydia sat frozen in place. She pulled her knees against her chest and wrapped her arms around them. She leaned against the wall for support, too scared to climb down from the protection of the loft. What if she did climb down and Joseph was lying in wait?

"Lydie? It's safe to come down."

"No." Her voice wavered. "Not right now. I'll come down in a bit. I want to make sure they're gone."

Wood creaked as Shane made his way up the ladder. He walked over to her side. "Are you okay?"

Tears of anger and fear overflowed from her eyes. "I hate him so much. He's turned this around and is putting all the blame on Ben. Ben wouldn't hurt anyone. He's the most gentle-hearted man I've ever met. He's taken care of me, and he'd never hurt me."

Shane sank down beside her. His strong presence made her feel safe and protected. The soothing aroma of fresh hay wafted her way as he settled in place.

Lydia looked up at him. "What if they find the cabin? Ben won't have a chance."

"They won't find him at the cabin. It's too remote. Just to show you how remote, I'll take you there after lunch. We'll check on Ben so you know he's okay."

"What about my brothers and sister?"

"After meeting your stepfather and his men, I think it's best if I meet him with the sheriff at my side. I'll send Gabriel to fetch him while we ride up the mountain."

"If the sheriff goes along, you'll be able to bring the children back with you for sure, won't you?"

"I can't make any promises that we'll get them right away, but I'll do the best I can. We can't break any laws in the process. I will get them back to you. We just have to tread carefully. The sheriff will know what to do."

A sense of peace flowed over her at his words. "I believe you. I'm going to pray that God provides a way for you to get them tomorrow."

"Your faith is inspiring." Shane stared at her from his place in the dusky loft. "I'm new to all this. Gabriel has explained enough to me, but I still don't understand it all. With everything that's happened to you, how have you kept your faith?"

"How could you not have kept yours?" Lydia countered. "With everything that's happened over the past few days, how can you not see God's hand in things?"

Shane smiled. "You have a good point. I'll contemplate that."

The sun shone through the cracks in the wood, highlighting the dust that floated between them.

She changed the subject. "You kissed me again just before you sent me up here."

"I did."

"You were the one saying we couldn't do that again."

"I know."

"Then why'd you do the opposite? And at such an inopportune time?"

"I kissed you so your scent would be on my clothes. The ruse worked. The dogs were thoroughly confused. They followed your scent in the barn, but it ended with me."

Lydia laughed. "I guess that's true. What a brilliant idea! I wondered what all that was about."

"Well now you know."

"Thank you." She wanted him to kiss her again. "For everything."

"You're welcome." Shane stared at her for a moment, then looked away. "I have a confession to make."

Lydia settled back against the rough-hewn wall and waited. She hoped he wasn't about to say he'd changed his mind about helping her. Though she had to admit, now that he'd seen Joseph in action, he had reason to rethink his involvement.

"What?" she asked warily.

He grinned at her. "I don't consider our kisses a mistake."

"Oh. You—don't?"

"No. I don't."

"What changed your mind?"

"I didn't have to kiss you before you climbed up in the loft. Your scent was already on my clothes from me holding you in my arms. I just wanted to check my emotions and see if kissing you really was a mistake or if it was something I enjoyed."

She raised an eyebrow. "You couldn't tell that from the kisses in the kitchen?"

"I wanted to be sure." He laughed. He ducked as she dropped a handful of hay on top of his dark curls.

"In all seriousness—why did you kiss me again?"

"I like kissing you. It's as simple as that." He settled back into place. "I'm not used to feeling that way. You have to understand. My father was a horrible husband to my mother, but my mother was a wonderful wife to him. The last time my father came home, he gave me a piece of advice, the only advice I ever remember him giving."

Lydia waited a moment, and when he didn't speak, she prompted him. "What was the advice?"

Shane looked at her long and hard. "He said for me to find a woman as good as my mother to marry and for me to stay away from his wandering ways."

"And you ignored him on both counts."

"I did." He nodded. "Right up until the other day when I saw you standing on the walkway in town. Something about you had my father's words coming back to me. You showed the same spirit as my mom. You were beautiful, intelligent, and courageous. You were fiercely protective of Wyatt. My mother would have been the same way. As a matter of fact, she would have cheered you on when you knocked that chair out from under me."

Lydia laughed in spite of her stress. "Oh, I doubt that."

"No, she absolutely would have. Then she would have grabbed me by the ear and hauled me out of the saloon."

He looked down. "My choice to follow my father into gambling would have been the biggest disappointment of her life."

Lydia was glad he couldn't see her face. She wasn't sure what to say in light of his confessions. "I doubt that would have been her biggest disappointment. Your father had to have broken her heart."

"And I would have broken it all over again."

"But you didn't. And now you're here, taking care of your sisters. The choice might have come late, but you've been given a second chance. It seems to me you're bent on taking it."

"I am." He sighed and pushed to his feet. He reached down to help her up. "I suppose we should go down now before tongues start wagging."

"I suppose you're right."

"Though if they're going to talk anyway, we might as well share one more kiss."

"You're incorrigible!" Lydia moved toward the ladder.

Shane grabbed her arm. "In the stories—stories like the one you just read to the girls—the fair maiden always rewards her rescuer with a kiss."

"I've already rewarded you with a few kisses too many."

"But this is a completely new rescue." He leaned nearer, and her heart did flips in her chest.

She leaned forward, too, and dropped her voice to a whisper. "And what would your mother have to say about you being alone in the loft with a woman who isn't your wife—*without* the benefit of a chaperone?"

He was close enough that she could feel his breath. "She'd probably tell me to do the proper thing and make the woman my wife."

Her heart skipped a beat. "And would you listen to her?"

"I'd probably listen to her about as well as I listened to my father."

The kiss never came. He smirked and moved away from

her and easily down the ladder.

The loft felt lonely without his presence. She hurried to follow him.

"As I said before"—he leaned close to her ear as she finished her descent—"no more kisses."

She buried her face in her hands and groaned. "You're the one who said I owed you a kiss!"

His blue eyes twinkled, teasing her. "And I think you might agree."

She thought she might agree, too. If she needed rescuing, which seemed to be quite often of late, Shane was the perfect hero to do so.

"Shane?" Gabriel's voice called from just outside the door.

They jumped guiltily apart.

"In here." Shane sent her an apologetic grin.

Gabriel entered the dim interior and looked back and forth between them. "It's safe to come out. I've been watching Joseph and his men from the attic. They headed back down to the plantation."

Shane stood in the doorway. "He's not happy."

"No, he isn't. We need to do something and fast."

"Lydia and I were just talking about options. I want to send for the sheriff."

Gabriel looked over at Lydia. She nodded her agreement.

"You need to stay here, Shane, in case they come back. I'll ride for the sheriff. Tildy has lunch on the table. She sent me to fetch you two."

"My thoughts exactly. I appreciate it, Gabe." Shane motioned for them to lead the way toward the house. He fell in behind them. "I'm taking Lydia up to visit Ben as soon as we've eaten. If you bring back the sheriff, we'll have everything in order, and we can ride out first thing in the morning."

fourteen

Lunch had been a quiet affair. No one wanted to talk about Joseph's visit with the children present. As soon as the girls excused themselves and ran out the back door, Shane leaned back in his chair. "They sure seem to be in a hurry to get outside."

"I told you they love it here." Gabriel smiled, watching them through the window. "It's the kind of place every child needs to grow up in. Plenty of fresh air. Lots of space. A nice, safe house."

"I get your point, Gabe." Shane softened his words with a partial smile. "And I agree. The girls love it here. I plan for them to stay."

Lydia's heart melted. She wanted the same for Wyatt. He'd thrive in a place like this. Though the plantation was roomy and had every comfort imaginable, it lacked the warmth of the homestead. And for the most part, no one but Joseph was allowed to enjoy the comforts. Wyatt's days were filled with chores and work in the fields. Joseph used every bit of help at his disposal, even the help of his children. Everyone at the plantation carried their weight—everyone but Joseph. Joseph paraded around and berated or disciplined anyone who didn't work up to his or her potential.

Shane placed his cloth napkin on the table. "Lydia and I are going to head up to the cabin and check on Ben. I want to make sure he has everything he needs."

"I'll put a basket together for him." Tildy hurried to her

feet and began gathering supplies.

Lydia walked over to help her.

"I'll ready the horses." Shane headed out the back door with Isaac and Gabriel on his heels.

The two women worked side by side and packed the basket full of muffins, eggs, jam, two loaves of bread, some butter, and a variety of cured meat. Tildy added a container of milk. "I hope he isn't lonely up there all alone."

"I would imagine he's relishing the quiet. Ben was born into slavery. He's never had the luxury of choosing how to spend his day." Lydia grew thoughtful. "Though I'm sure he'd enjoy it more if Sadie was at his side. He won't rest until he has her with him."

"I can't imagine being separated from Isaac." Tildy clucked. "We worked the same plantation together, grew up side by side. We had a kind master who let us marry and live as husband and wife. He gave us our freedom, but most of us chose to stay on and continue as we were."

"What changed?" Lydia couldn't imagine slave owners who were so kind. She'd only known the harsh ways of her stepfather and his friends. "What made you leave?"

"Our master passed away, and his wife wanted to sell. She gave us plenty of warnin', though, and we were able to contact Gabe. He suggested we come here and take care of Shane's place for him." She smiled. "It was in horrible disarray. We both worked long, hard days and enjoyed every minute. The first structure we rebuilt was the cabin—the one Ben's living in now."

"I look forward to seeing it."

"I believe you'll enjoy its charm. We lived there while fixing up the house and barn." She wiped her hands on the skirt of her apron and glanced around the kitchen. "I suppose we have everything Ben will need for now."

"He'll think this a feast fit for a king. As you've seen, my stepfather wasn't a good man. His slaves—his *workers*," she said, her voice laced with sarcasm, "weren't treated very well, and they were fed even worse. Ben and the others have lived a very harsh life. There wasn't anything I could do to make things better."

"I can imagine." Tildy laid her hand on Lydia's shoulder. "His choices aren't your burdens to carry."

Lydia sighed. "I know. But it's hard to let go of a lifetime of guilt. While I walked around in my beautiful clothes, Joseph treated us all horribly, but we had to make a good impression on his friends who would drop by without warning—the other girls my age on the plantation wore nothing but rags. We ate till our bellies were full, even though the best food went to Joseph. We never went hungry like the slaves."

"That was Joseph's choice, child, and he alone will pay the price for his sins."

"I suppose you're right."

"I am and don't you forget it." She cupped Lydia's cheek and grinned. "You get on up there and take your friend his food."

"Yes'm." Lydia picked up the basket. "And you have fun with the girls."

"I fully intend to. We have cookies to make."

"They'll love that, Tildy." Lydia looked out the window where Isaac was hanging a swing made of ropes and a board on a sturdy branch in the girls' favorite tree. All three clapped their hands with excitement and anticipation.

"We've only been here two days, and already the girls are blooming."

"Um-hum. I'd imagine we're in for some tough times with

Emma after the new wears off and she starts missing her mama." Tildy tsked at the thought. "But we'll rally and be here for her when that time comes."

"We will," Lydia agreed. "I mean, if I get to stay on."

"Shane ain't sendin' you nowhere, Miss Lydie."

"I hope you're right. This place is as soothing for my soul as it seems to be for theirs."

They watched Isaac put Lucy on the swing and gently give it a push. She squealed with terrified glee. Savannah and Emma jumped up and down, vying for a turn. Isaac helped Lucy off, and Emma took her place. Savannah bounced with excited energy. When Savannah finally got her turn, Gabe and Shane walked toward the house with Chester and Pal.

"Looks like it's time for me to go."

"Have fun, Lydia. You deserve to."

"I'll have fun after I get my family to safety."

"Your siblings' situation ain't gonna change just because you're mopin' around worryin' about them. Have some fun. There's nothin' you can do for them right now. Enjoy this time with Shane."

"That's a good way to look at it, Tildy." Lydia gave the older woman a spontaneous hug. "You give good advice. Thank you. I know our arrival must have turned your peaceful world upside down. Yet you've been nothing but kind and gracious to us."

"I love my Isaac and his company, Miss Lydie, but when y'all arrived here yesterday, our whole world lit up like the sunrise. We've been mighty lonely after all this time on our own. We grew up in the company of friends, and we're more than ready to share our time with others." She swatted at Lydia with her towel. "Now go on with ya while I try to compete with Isaac and the swing for the girls' company."

Lydia stepped out the door and was greeted by Shane's crooked smile. "Ready?"

"I think so. Tildy and I packed enough food to feed a family for a week."

Tildy opened the door. "I slipped a couple of sandwiches in so y'all could have a picnic if you're late gettin' home."

Lydia flushed. Tildy didn't even try to be subtle.

Shane helped her up onto Chester, secured the basket of food, and swung up onto Pal. "Let's go."

He took off at a trot, and Lydia fell into place behind him. She studied him as they rode. He sat tall and straight in the saddle. His black hair peeked out from under his hat and curled at his collar. From the back he looked like an Indian warrior sitting confidently atop his palomino.

They headed into the woods at the base of the mountain and began to climb. The trail was barely noticeable, and if Shane hadn't been in the lead, Lydia would never have seen it. The branches and scrub tugged at their clothes. Shane stopped and thoughtfully held back the longest of limbs so Lydia wouldn't be hurt by their backlash, protecting her just as he had in the barn.

She'd badly misjudged him at the saloon. The man she'd met that day had been hurting and trying to find his way, just as she'd tried to find hers all these years while under Joseph's hand. Now they were both free to discover who they were. Shane had found his place by returning home while Lydia found hers by leaving.

The trail began to climb, and Lydia focused on her surroundings. The rugged hillside beauty was nothing like the flatter land of her home. She'd seen the mountains from afar, but never had she found the time to go exploring.

A bubbling stream flanked the trail for a time, and Lydia

slowed when the trail widened. She drifted over to the beautiful space and stopped in the middle of a clearing. She wanted nothing more than to settle down on the luscious grass that grew beside the brook and watch the water rush over the pebbles.

"You'll have plenty of time to linger after we visit Ben and rescue Wyatt." Shane's chuckle from behind her caused her to start.

She glanced back at him. "The only time I've ever been in the hills was when my stepfather ordered the men to leave me two nights ago. It's so beautiful here. I never even knew something like this existed."

Shane looked at her, contemplative.

"What?" She grew self-conscious.

He turned his horse back to the trail. "Follow me. I want to show you something."

She urged Chester to follow him. Their trail wound around the side of the mountain now. After another mile, Shane swung to the ground. He secured the horses to a nearby branch where they could reach the stream for a drink or snack on the abundant grass.

"We have to walk from here." He reached for her hand.

"To get to the cabin?"

"No, to get to the place I want to show you."

She took his hand, and they worked their way through the dense underbrush for what seemed an eternity. Lydia couldn't imagine what was worth the scratches and rough terrain.

Finally they stepped into an open space that ended in a ledge. Lydia looked out over the expanse, and the view took her breath away. "It's—it's absolutely beautiful."

"It is. I thought you'd like it."

The valley spread below them, and in the far distance she

could see the plantation home where she'd grown up. Tears filled her eyes. "Wyatt's down there somewhere, wondering where I've gone, wondering why I've abandoned him."

Shane pulled her into his arms. "I bet he's tougher than you think. He knows you'll return for him." His strong hands caressed her hair.

Lydia laid her head on his shoulder and let him hold her close. She pulled strength from his nearness. "This is what you wanted to show me?"

"Yes." He moved away from her and led her closer to the edge. "I spent so many boyhood hours in this place. I loved the view from here, and I'd often imagine who the people were that lived in such a magnificent house."

"Our house."

"Yes." He stood with arms crossed and feet spread. He looked like he owned the world. "You said back at the stream that you'd grown up here and had never known the beauty of the mountains."

"Right."

He sent her a smile. "I grew up in the mountains and never knew the beauty growing up in the house I'd watched over from afar."

"Oh. Um—" Lydia didn't know how to respond to such a blatant compliment. "Thank you."

"You're welcome."

They stood and studied the plantation for a few more moments.

"We need to be going." Shane took her elbow and turned her from the view.

She looked over her shoulder for one last glance, wishing she could see Wyatt. "Thank you for sharing this with me."

"I have a lot of other things I'd love to show you and

experience with you after all of this is over. That is, if you'll let me."

"You have to ask? I'd love to have you show me all of it!" Her heart trilled. He wanted to see her after he helped her. "Wyatt would love it up here."

"Then we'll start by bringing the kids for a picnic here on the ledge. Maybe let them have a swim in the stream."

"Wyatt has never experienced such a thing. We've had impromptu picnics in our yard, back when my mother was alive—on the rare occasions when Joseph would go to town. I'm not sure about him being up here with the ledge, though. He's so impulsive."

"So was I, Mama Bear. He'll be fine. I'll make sure of it."

"All right."

"You're gonna love it here, Lydia. It's a great place for a boy like Wyatt to grow up." He took her hand, and his deep blue eyes peered into hers. "I hope you'll stay on after we get the kids, at least for a while, once Joseph is taken care of. I'll understand if you want to return home at some point if Joseph ends up in jail. But I want you to know that Wyatt, Nathan, and Natalie are welcome to stay with us for as long as you want."

Lydia blinked back the tears that threatened to fall. It was official. They had a place to go, a place that wasn't the plantation. "I'll never want to go back there if I have a choice."

"You have a choice."

"Thank you. I'd like to stay, at least for a while."

His eyes clouded for a moment. "I know we've just met, but I hope you'll consider staying on for more than a while. Take the time you need to heal. Take the time to figure out where you want to be." He leaned down to give her a gentle kiss. A kiss that carried a world of promise. "It took me four long years to realize I'd already been to the place I wanted to be. I had to explore the countryside to appreciate what I had here at home."

"I can already tell you I don't need to go anywhere else. It's beautiful and peaceful here." Peaceful was the only requirement she had.

Shane laughed. "Peaceful? With three little girls and Wyatt on the way? Throw in the twins and you'll have anything but peaceful."

"Peaceful and quiet are two different things, Shane. I never said it would be quiet. Peaceful is a place deep inside your soul. A place deep within my soul anyway. I've never experienced it before now."

His expression turned teasing. "I think that's what I felt right up until you fell out of that tree and landed on my lap. Savannah had been nagging me about finding a wife and settling down so we could stay at the homestead." He glanced at her. "If you haven't noticed, she's very persistent."

"I've noticed."

"I told her if God wanted me to have a wife, He'd have to drop her on my lap."

"And there I was."

"Yes. There you were. There's no stopping Savannah now. She's sure God sent you to us."

Lydia turned back to the view. "And what do you think?"

He was silent for so long she turned around to make sure he still stood beside her. "I think God has a plan for all of us, and I think God's central to that plan."

"I agree. I've always had faith. I don't know how I'd have made it through the past few years without it. But you—your faith is new, isn't it?"

He nodded. "I was raised up to have faith, but I pushed it away after I lost my mother. Gabriel made it his life's quest to bring me back to that faith."

"It worked."

"It did. In an unexpected way and when I least expected it."

"That's how God works." Lydia gave him an impish smile. "And how life works, too. If you aren't careful, you'll be stuck with us forever."

"I can think of worse things than that."

"Wyatt can be a handful. I know you've seen that, but he can really take a toll on a person's nerves."

"Sounds like me when I was young."

Lydia laughed. "I can only imagine."

fifteen

They walked back to the waiting horses and continued their climb. The path turned and zigzagged the opposite direction until they entered another clearing. A small cabin sat in the midst of the open area. A cozy porch ran across the front of the house.

Lydia hurried Chester forward and slid down from his back. "Ben!"

She expected the front door to burst open, but it didn't. She continued forward, leading Chester along behind her. Shane pulled up and reached for the reins.

"Thank you." She smiled at him and hurried up the steps. "Ben?" She knocked on the door.

Heavy footsteps moved across the room from the other side of the door.

"Ben, it's me, Lydia."

The door opened wide, and a huge grin spread across his wrinkled face.

"Miz Lydie! You be lookin' much better than last time I saw ya."

Lydia laughed. "It's hasn't been such a long time. Only a day."

"You still be lookin' better. You rested, and the bruises done faded."

"She was worried about you." Shane stepped up beside her, having secured the horses.

"Now Miz Lydie, why you go worryin' 'bout an ole man like me?"

Lydia looked at Shane.

He nodded and pointed at the chairs that stood in a row on the porch. "Let's sit down."

"Joseph came to the homestead today."

Ben's features wrinkled with concern. "He didn't find out you wuz there?"

"No," she hurried to reassure him. "But he was angry, and he's pinning my whole disappearance on you. He told Shane and Isaac that you kidnapped me and disappeared. Ben, you have to be careful. If they find you—"

"I've done had my taste of freedom, Miz Lydie. The only place I'm goin' when I leave this mountain is to find my precious Sadie. Joseph and his men ain't gonna stop me."

"Gabriel has gone for the sheriff. Let us take care of Joseph before you leave here. I don't want to take any chances. Joseph's men had a lot of guns today. You wouldn't stand a chance if you ran into them. They'd shoot first and explain later. We need you alive and well."

Ben started to disagree.

"Sadie needs you alive and well," said Shane.

Ben couldn't argue with that. Lydia sent Shane a thankful smile and turned back to Ben. "We brought you some food."

Shane went down the steps two at a time and retrieved the basket.

Ben shook his head. "Tildy done packed me a hamper yesterday. I ain't begun to eat it. How can she expect me to eat all this food? Have y'all eaten?"

Shane nodded. "We did before we started up here, but I'll take a muffin."

"Miz Lydie? You wanna a muffin?"

"Sure."

Lydia figured if they kept him distracted, he'd forget about going after Sadie. She picked a muffin from the basket and leaned back to nibble on it while the men talked. It was the first time she'd paid attention to the view from the porch.

"Oh, Shane, it's beautiful up here." She stopped with the muffin half raised to her lips, mesmerized. They were halfway up the mountain, and the cleared trees allowed a view that looked out over the distant mountains. Rolling hill after rolling hill went on for as far as she could see. "I feel like I can see all the way to Atlanta!"

Shane laughed. "You could if we were facing south. We've traveled around enough that we're actually facing northwest. These are small hills compared to the mountains north of us, but they do make for a pretty view, don't they?"

"Breathtaking. I had no idea. I could sit on this porch forever."

"That works fine for me, Miz Lydie. You sit up here and stay safe while enjoyin' the view, and I'll go down the mountain with Shane to settle things up with Joseph and his men. I s'pose it'll do him good to see me face-to-face while he's telling the sheriff his lies."

Lydia sat up straight in her chair, the muffin dangling in her fingers. "You'll do no such thing! And neither shall I. I refuse to sit here while everyone else is down there fighting my battle."

"It's my battle, too, Miz Lydie," Ben said quietly. "Joseph made this my battle the day slavery ended and he didn't give us our freedom. He made it another battle when he took away my Sadie. Now he's settin' me up for a kidnappin' charge I never committed."

Tears filled Lydia's eyes. "I understand, but I don't like it."

"I don't much like it either, child, but we be all right. We have the good Lord on our side, and ain't no one gonna hurt us. I got to go along. Joseph'll have his guns and men, but we also be havin' guns and men. If I's there, we be gettin' the cooperation of the others. They need me, Lydie."

The tears rolled freely down Lydia's cheeks. It was the first time he'd sounded grandfatherly. The chains that had bound his spirit were falling off.

"I see that they do, Ben." She wiped at the tears with the palm of her hand. "But I'm going down the mountain, too. As beautiful as it is up here, I'm not staying alone. Shane's already said I can't go along to the plantation, but I want to be as close to the action as I can. If y'all bring Wyatt back, I want to be there to hold him."

"You watch for us, Miz Lydie. I'll bring Wyatt back to you. You know he'll come with me."

"That he will."

Shane stood and paced the length of the porch. "We plan to bring everyone back if we can, Ben—the workers, Wyatt, and the twins. We won't know the details until we get back to the house."

"Do you think Gabe and the sheriff are back?" Lydia wanted to get going if so. The nearer they were to making the final plan, the nearer they were to getting Wyatt safely in her arms.

"I doubt it. Gabe took the shorter route through the back side of the plantation, but it'll take him the better part of the afternoon and evening to get there and back. There's no road, but the path should get him there fast enough."

Ben intervened. "What 'bout Joseph's men? They patrol the back end o' the farthest cotton field."

"He'll stay on our property. Joseph's men won't catch him."

"I don't see no reason for us to sit up here talkin' when we can make our way down the mountain." Ben stood. "I'll grab my things, and we be ready to go."

Lydia joined Shane and rested her forearms on the porch rail. "It's unbelievably beautiful. I didn't think it could get any prettier than down at the stream. Then you showed me the ledge—now this."

"The beauty is unending."

Lydia looked up at him, ready to agree, but she realized he was staring at her. Her mouth quirked in a self-conscious grin. "Are we talking about the same thing? The beauty of the mountainside?"

"More or less." He laughed. "I'm learning there are many different kinds of beauty in these hills."

"Hmm." She glanced back out over the valley, furrowing her forehead.

"We'll come back up here with the children, too. They'll like it. Savannah and Lucy don't remember any of this. I'll enjoy seeing our mountain through their eyes."

"Maybe Wyatt won't be so wild if he has all this within reach. I bet we can tire him out really well."

"I'd imagine, now that you mention it, that's the exact reason why my mother allowed us boys to run the hills so much in our youth."

"I'm sure you're right."

"I'm glad she got to enjoy Savannah for the first four years of her life. Mama had her hands full of us boys."

❧

Shane enjoyed the trip down the mountain enough that he again chose the longer route. Ben started to question him as they rode out, but Shane silenced him with a nod. Ben looked at Lydia, who sat in front of Shane on Pal, and gave him a knowing grin.

Shane knew Lydia would find out about the more direct

route down to the homestead soon enough, but he'd enjoyed their trip up, and he intended to prolong their trip down. Gabe wouldn't be back until just before nightfall, so they had no reason to rush.

He savored the scent of her sun-warmed hair. She smelled fresh like spring. He wished the bruises and cut would fade away so he'd not be reminded of the trauma she'd experienced after he met her in town. He wished he could wipe it all away. He remembered standing in the middle of the street in town, watching her walk away, watching as she climbed onto the wagon with Wyatt, and watching her round the corner.

He'd wanted to go after her. Gabriel had walked up and in one look had known Shane had lost his heart.

"I should have gone after you." He whispered the words into her hair.

"What?" Lydia turned a bit in his arms.

"That day in town, after we left the saloon, I wanted to chase you down."

"Oh."

He didn't blame her for the surprise in her voice. "You were so angry, and I didn't like the way it made me feel. I watched you stalk away. I wanted to make you come back, to make things right. I didn't want you upset with me."

"You didn't even know me."

"My heart did. Somehow. Though I didn't understand it then."

They were nearing the main path to the house. Ben moved around them and headed in as Shane slowed. "I know it's only been a couple of days. But that moment, standing there on the dirt of the road, I might as well have been hit by a bolt of lightning. That's how mesmerizing the moment was for me."

"I'd just knocked you flat on your back." Lydia laughed. "You must have hit your head."

"No. My senses were fully intact." He enjoyed her sense of humor.

"And then I fell on your lap from the tree. Are you sure you can stand having me around? It could prove to be very dangerous."

Dangerous to my foolish heart, he thought.

"After facing off with Joseph tomorrow, spending time getting to know you will be most enjoyable." He laughed.

"I'm glad you think so."

Ben was heading into the stable as they rode into the yard. Shane swung off Pal and reached up to help Lydia.

"Lydie! Lydie! Lydie!" A chorus of voices called out moments before the girls burst through the back door. They threw their arms around her.

"We missed you." Lucy's words were muffled against the skirt of Lydia's dress.

Lydia pulled the other two girls slightly away so the child could breathe as she looked laughingly over at Shane. "So I see."

"You were gone a long time," Emma said solemnly.

"Not really," Lydia corrected. "We were only gone for the better part of the afternoon. You haven't even had the evening meal, have you?"

"No."

"What about me?" Shane inserted, wanting to give Lydia a break. "Didn't anyone miss me?"

Savannah rolled her eyes. "We've always had you around."

Shane raised his eyebrows. "Oh really? That wasn't what you said when I saw you yesterday morning! You said it was about time I'd come back to get you. And"—he moved slowly forward—"I believe it's about time I get you right now."

A moment later realization dawned on Savannah's face. "No!"

She tripped backward in her hurry to get away from him. Emma and Lucy clung to Lydia's skirt, their faces apprehensive. He winked at them. Lucy gave him a shy smile, but Emma still looked worried. Lydia swung her up into her arms.

"Yes." He crept closer.

Savannah was scrambling backward on her hands and feet and laughing. She couldn't move fast enough to get away from him. He dove forward and tickled her until she could hardly breathe.

"Tickle me! Tickle me!" Lucy jumped on his back. He swung around on his hands and knees, spinning until she lost her grip. Her giggles were contagious. Even Emma joined in the laughter. He caught Lucy with his arm and used the other to tickle Savannah some more.

"Miss me now, Van?"

"No! Not when you're tickling me!"

"Admit it, you like the attention."

Emma wiggled down and crept closer. Lydia stayed close to her side. Shane reached up and tickled the little girl until she laughed out loud. She jumped on his back, and the other two joined in, trying to hold him down. In the end he let them win.

They ran off to the swing, and he sat on his knees watching them, breathing hard. Isaac had come for Pal while Shane played with the girls.

"You just gained Emma's trust." Lydia smiled.

"I believe you're right. And Savannah let her guard down."

Lydia held out a hand to help him to his feet. "She was pretty upset with you from what I understood. She's missed you."

"I don't know what I was thinking. I've missed so much of their lives."

"And now you'll be here to experience so much more."

"You always see the good, don't you?"

"I try."

Gabe rode into the yard with a stranger. He hadn't brought the sheriff. Shane dusted off his clothes as he walked over to greet them.

"Shane, this is Duncan." Shane shook the man's hand and waited for Gabe's explanation. "The sheriff couldn't come, he has a problem in town, but he deputized Duncan a while back and sent him in his place."

"This won't be easy—"

"Gabriel filled us in on everything," Duncan interrupted. "I've worked with the sheriff on several other occasions. I feel confident I'll be able to handle things."

"Good." Relief washed over Shane. He didn't want their plans to fall apart. "I'm glad to meet you, Deputy."

"Duncan is fine."

Tildy called everyone in for supper. Shane looked over at the girls. "You girls want to have a picnic?"

They ran inside to wash up while Lydia went in for a blanket. Tildy said she'd plate up their meals. Shane saw the lilt in Lydia's step as she carried the blanket over to the girls. She shook it, and the ends of the linen flew high into the air. It drifted slowly to the ground. Lydia bent to smooth the edges.

Shane felt like the piece of linen. Lydie's arrival had shaken him up, too, and now her presence smoothed his rough edges. Tomorrow would end Lydia's trauma, and hopefully by the end of the day, Wyatt would be safely in her arms. His displaced belle might change her mind and be more than happy to stay at the plantation after everything leveled out. He wouldn't blame her if she changed her mind. With Joseph safely behind bars—the best scenario for him—Lydie might realize her place is in her family home. Shane knew she wouldn't be far, even if she did decide to return to her family home. Their boundaries touched, and he could court her from afar. But he desperately hoped she'd decide to stay with them. Regardless, the deputy's arrival had set the plan into motion.

sixteen

Shane sat on his horse and surveyed the five ladies lined up before him. He had a feeling this image would be forever burned into his memory. He'd already told the women to stay alert and to keep their weapons within reach.

Lydia held Emma on her hip. Lydia's features were strained and her eyes full of concern. He tried to convey through his confidence that everything would be fine. Emma lay with her head on Lydia's shoulder. Though young, she obviously felt the nervous tension. Tildy held Lucy, who was reaching and crying for Shane. The older woman rocked his little sister in her arms, crooning softly in her ear.

Tildy nodded her head at Shane and waved him on, assuring him she had everything under control. Savannah, looking half-grown, stood between the two women, courage and concern warring across her features. Shane knew she wanted to be strong for him, but at the same time he could see she wanted nothing more than to throw herself into his arms.

"I'm going to be fine, Van. We'll come home as soon as we can."

A lone tear rolled down Savannah's cheek as concern won out. She nodded, her voice lost in a sob.

Tildy wrapped her free arm around Savannah's shoulder at the same time that Lydia took the little girl's hand.

"We know you're goin' to be fine." Tildy voiced her faith. "We're goin' to be prayin' the entire time y'all are gone, aren't we girls?"

"I'm glad to hear it." Shane looked them over one last time and turned his horse to follow the other men. The deputy led the way into the trees, the others falling in single file. Shane brought up the rear.

"I love you, Shane!" Savannah's panicked voice suddenly broke the silence as she chased him into the trees.

He pulled his horse to a stop and turned around. "I know you do, Van. I love you, too."

A tiny smile shaped her mouth as she nodded. Lydia called her back, and Savannah hurried to obey.

The ride to the plantation was a quiet one. No one wanted to chance warning Joseph's men of their arrival. They'd discussed it the night before and felt catching everyone off-guard would be the best way to go.

Ben motioned for them to stop. "This here is the outskirts of the western corner."

The deputy nodded and slowly moved forward. They stopped just inside the tree line to study the situation.

Shane pulled up alongside the deputy. After a few moments, he quietly asked, "What do you think?"

Pal shifted beneath him, his movements antsy. Two horses down, Chester snorted.

Duncan adjusted the front of his hat. "I think we should ride out of the trees as we are. Keep your rifles at the ready, but don't point them at anyone unless necessary. Let me take the lead and listen for my direction."

The men murmured in agreement.

"Let's go."

They moved casually from the trees, and for a couple of minutes, no one noticed their arrival.

Shane scoured the field, locating Wyatt at once. He bent over the crop right alongside everyone else, his features tired and strained. A younger version of Lydia worked at his side. Natalie. She reached over and caressed the little boy's head. Wyatt appeared to be in good hands.

One of the hands on horseback started their way. The others fell in behind him.

"Can I help you?" This boy was just shy of adulthood. His size and features put him at the right age to be Lydia's other brother, Nathan.

"We're here to talk to Joseph."

"He's not available at the moment, but you can talk to me."

"We really need to talk to Joseph."

The men behind Nathan nervously shifted their shotguns.

A burly man pushed ahead of Nathan. "The boy's made it clear Joseph isn't here. Y'all need to be on your way."

Nathan scowled, not happy with the man's pushiness. "I'm handling things."

"We can wait." Duncan wasn't going to be put off. "We'll head over to the plantation house and make ourselves at home."

Shane noticed one of the riders had moved away and was now riding full speed toward the house. He nodded toward the rider. "Looks like someone is going to get Joseph for us."

The other men looked over their shoulders, and the burly man swore.

Wyatt was looking their way, and Shane pulled his hat lower over his face. The last thing he needed was for the boy to recognize him from town and make a scene. The workers had stopped their progress. Natalie nervously wiped her hands on her skirt, staring their way. Shane saw her mouth Ben's name. Her face hardened. Shane wondered if Joseph had spread the same rumors about Ben to Lydia's family and the workers. If so, it would be harder to gain their trust.

Two riders were heading their direction from the far side of the field. Shane recognized Joseph as they neared.

"What are you men doing on my property?" he bellowed.

"Same thing you were doing on their property when you paid them your friendly little visit yesterday," Duncan drawled. "The way I hear it, you threatened these folks and said you'd return."

"I just asked them some questions," Joseph hedged. He glanced along the line of men and noticed Ben. His eyes went wide as he pointed a shaky finger in Ben's direction. "If you want to question someone, why don't you ask that man right there what he did with my daughter?"

"This man didn't have anything to do with your daughter's disappearance."

Ben's quiet voice joined in. "But I can tell you who did." He looked over at the burly man and his partner.

The burly man paled. "You can't prove anything with your empty threats."

"I shore enough can, and Miz Lydia will testify, too."

"She survived?" The smaller man backed his horse away. "I don't want no trouble. We was only followin' orders. Joseph ordered us to take her away."

"Shut up!" Joseph snarled. "They're bluffing. They don't know where Lydia is any more than we do."

The man cringed, wrapping his fingers nervously into his horse's mane.

"If that's true, why are you blaming Ben for her disappearance? Your man there pretty much gave me a confession just now."

"Idiot," Joseph snarled under his breath. His words slurred.

The numbers were pretty even. Besides Joseph, Nathan, the burly man, and his scrawny partner, there were only two others. Shane calculated their odds if everyone went for their weapons.

Nathan, according to Lydia, wouldn't engage in any shooting. Not unless he was sure he was fighting on the right side. From his expression of distaste, he didn't think the right side would include Joseph.

Joseph would shoot, but based on his slurred speech and his alcohol-scented aroma, his aim would be poor due to drinking. The scrawny man was shaking too hard to pull a trigger. That left the burly man and the two others to their five.

"Ben, did you have anything you wanted to say?" Duncan asked.

"I do." He looked over at the workers. "Joseph sent Lydia away with these two"—he waved toward the culprits with two fingers—"two days ago. He instructed them to do whatever they wanted with her, as long as they made sure she didn't ever return."

Nathan's eyes narrowed. "Is this true?"

Joseph's laugh was sinister. "None of your business, boy."

"It is my business."

Duncan moved closer to Joseph.

An instant later, paranoia swept across Joseph's features. "You ain't taking me away. I have family and responsibilities to tend to. Y'all get off my property and don't bother coming back."

Duncan looked over at the workers. "Are any of you working of your own volition? Are you here by choice?" A few of the workers glanced at each other, but most merely looked down at the ground. "If you're being held here by force, I'm giving you the chance to leave right now."

A few of the faces filled with hope.

Shane noticed that Natalie had moved closer, her hand protectively on Wyatt's shoulder. Both had fresh bruises on their faces. Shane looked at Nathan and noticed he favored his left arm. Joseph had been a very busy man. And a very angry man.

Ben looked over his people. "Please. You'll be safe with us if you leave right now. Joseph can't hurt you now that the law is involved."

Shane saw desire war with terror, but finally several of the workers stepped forward.

"Is it true?" Wyatt's quiet voice asked. "Is Lydia with you?" Wyatt looked hopeful, then burst into tears. "I want Lydie!"

Natalie pulled him close against her skirt.

"It's true," Shane stated. "Lydia's fine. She sent us to get you."

"You ain't takin' my kids anywhere."

Duncan raised a hand. "I'm taking them. I have a responsibility to see to their safety, and with the fresh signs of abuse on their faces, I'm taking them with us."

"You can't do that!" Joseph's expression was wild.

None of the workers dared move.

"I can, and I am."

"It's not legal."

"We can figure all that out in town at the sheriff's office."

"You ain't taking me to any sheriff." He spun his horse around and looked at his men. "Take care of them!"

He hurried off, but Duncan didn't show any sign of chasing him. Instead he targeted the other four men with his glare.

"I ain't doing nothin'," the scrawny one said. He threw his rifle to the ground. "He don't pay us enough for the things he wants us to do."

"I agree." The burly one kept his firearm, but he spun

around and headed toward the far side of the property, away from both the plantation and Shane's spread. The scrawny guy followed along. It only took a moment for the last two to follow suit.

"Nathan?" Duncan asked.

"Yes, sir."

"Are you going to 'take care of us'?"

"I am, sir." He turned his horse to face his sister and brother. "Natalie? Wyatt? Prepare to ride out with the men here."

Duncan laughed. "I'm not sure that's exactly what your stepfather had in mind."

Nathan's grin matched the deputy's. "I don't reckon it is, but it's what we're doing."

Wyatt's face lit up. "You're the man from the saloon!"

Shane cringed. "I am, but I'm not ever stepping foot in a saloon again. God and Lydia have changed my ways."

"I wanna ride with the brave man. Please, Nathan? Lydie knocked him flat on his back. He was really mad."

Nathan's eyes narrowed.

"It's a long story," Shane hurried to say. "I can assure you, your sister has made her peace with me."

"Um-hum, according to Tildy, she sure has." Isaac spoke for the first time.

Gabriel's mouth dropped open, and he stared from Isaac to Shane. "What haven't you told me, Shane? What's all this, 'Um-hum, she sure has' stuff?"

"Tildy caught them kissing in the kitchen yesterday morning."

"You kissed my sister?" Nathan's gun raised a notch. "After only knowing her one day?"

Shane wondered if Lydia had underestimated her younger brother.

"It's not how it sounds. I can explain. But this is hardly the place."

"He's right," Duncan interrupted. "We need to be going. I want to get the kids settled in before dark."

"Lydia's going to be worried if we don't hurry up and get back to her. We'll explain everything when we get there."

Natalie reached up to touch Nathan's leg. "Please, Nathan. I don't want to spend another night here. Let's get going."

Her plea seemed to center him. "Okay, Wyatt, you ride with—what did you say your name is?"

"I didn't. The name's Shane. I own the land behind the plantation and the better part of that mountain." Shane reached down, and Wyatt grabbed his hand. Shane pulled him up and settled him in the circle of Shane's arms.

"Good to meet you." Nathan reached a hand to Natalie and swung her up onto the horse behind him. "I'm Nathan, and this is my sister, Natalie."

"Lydia's told us all about you."

"Let's get out of here," Duncan said. He looked over at the workers. "We'll move slowly, and you all can keep up on foot. I'm sorry we don't have a better way. It's not safe for you to remain behind."

"They are good people," Ben reassured. "Let 'em help you."

"What about Joseph and the men who left Miss Lydie to—" Isaac glanced over at Wyatt and tempered his words as he voiced the question everyone had to have on their mind. "Who left Miss Lydia in the woods? Shouldn't we go after them?"

"No, the sheriff told me to get the kids and workers to safety. He said he'd put a posse together if he needed to and would round up whoever needed roundin'."

Duncan turned to Shane and Nathan. "You two ride ahead

and give the women some peace. They're going to worry until they have news. You'll have time to reunite everyone and to let Tildy know there'll be about a dozen extra people for dinner before we arrive at the house."

Shane looked over at Gabe and Isaac. Both nodded their agreement.

"Don't do anything crazy," Shane admonished them. "I don't want to face Tildy or Lydia's wrath if something happens to either one of you."

"Nothing's going to happen, Shane. We'll be fine." Gabriel grinned. It wasn't often he got to stay around for the finale while Shane missed out. Shane usually *was* the finale.

"I'll bring up the rear. If Joseph tries anything, he'll have me to deal with," stated Duncan.

Shane felt secure knowing Duncan had everything under control.

❧

Lydia paced the clearing. She'd circled the open area at least a hundred times while keeping an eye on the girls. Tildy stayed inside the house, cooking up a storm. She said she had complete faith that God would protect and bring the entire plantation's worth of workers home.

Lydia had explained that the plantation only had a handful of workers. She passed by the back door. Tildy opened the door and stepped out onto the porch. "No sign yet?"

"Nothing." She wrapped her arms around her waist. "What's keeping them, Tildy? It's been longer than they expected. What if—"

"Huh-uh, honey. You aren't goin' there. We aren't going to think the worst. We're gonna keep on prayin' and wait to see how God answers. His ways are always best, right?"

"You're right." Lydia sighed. "I guess I'll continue to—"

"Shane!" Savannah screeched.

Lydia spun around to see the three girls running toward the trees. Shane rode their way with Wyatt nestled in his arms. Lydia pressed her shaking hands over her mouth as tears poured down her face. "Wyatt!"

The words were barely a whispered sob, too soft for Wyatt to hear.

"Is that your other brother and sister behind him? God's answered our prayers, Lydia. He's brought your family home."

Lydia nodded, still not able to speak. She moved forward toward the happy group. The two littlest girls danced dangerously close to Pal's legs. Shane shooed them away, but they didn't listen. They wanted to be close to Shane.

Shane gave up. He stopped the horse and waited for Lydia to join them. She was crying so hard she could barely walk.

"I told you I'd bring them home."

"Lydie!" Wyatt's and Natalie's voices merged. Nathan sat on his horse and grinned at her.

"I've missed you all so much!" Lydia reached for Wyatt and wrapped him in her embrace. He clung to her neck and cried. "I told you I'd come back. I came this far and couldn't get to the plantation, so Shane volunteered to go the rest of the way for me."

"I told you he was brave." Wyatt sniffled.

"You were right." She exchanged a happy, watery smile with Shane. She turned to her sister. "Natalie. Nathan. I'm so glad you got away." Nathan and Natalie jumped down, and they all hugged.

"Where are the others?" she asked Shane as they walked toward the house. The little girls had already snagged Natalie and were dragging her over to the tree. Wyatt wouldn't leave Lydia's arms, and she was glad. She wasn't ready to let go of his warm little body.

"They're coming up behind us," Shane explained. "Or at least they were. They're with the workers who are traveling here on foot."

They stopped at the porch steps.

"Tildy, we'll have another dozen or so people for dinner. I was told to warn you."

"Oh my goodness. I'd best get back to work."

"I'll help." Lydia started up the steps.

"Nonsense." Tildy waved her towel. "You'll go visit with your family. You know I have things under control."

Nathan took his horse and Pal to the barn. Natalie went in to help him. The girls trailed at her heels.

"Your family settles right in." Shane led her to a bench.

"They do. You'll like them. Nathan's a hard worker, and Natalie will love helping Tildy in the kitchen." Wyatt rested on her shoulder. Lydia could feel his sweet breath blowing against her neck. "He's exhausted. And he has a bruise on his cheek."

"I saw."

"What did they do with Joseph?"

Shane hesitated.

"Tell me."

"He ran off. Duncan said the sheriff will put together a posse to find him and the two men who left you in the woods."

Panic flared. "He'll not give up, Shane. He hates to lose. He'll come back for us."

"He won't get you. Duncan's staying over, and we'll have a barn full of men to help. We'll assign people to watch over the yard in shifts as everyone else sleeps. We won't let anything happen to you."

Lydia knew she wouldn't sleep a wink. She'd make sure her siblings slept in the room with her. She knew Nathan would insist on doing his share of the watch.

"Duncan told me last night that once they have everything finished up here, they'll locate Sadie and bring her back to Ben."

"I'm glad to hear that."

Gabe interrupted, bursting from the trees at a fast pace. He saw Lydia and tried to gain his composure. "I need to speak to you, Shane."

Lydia stayed Shane with her hand. "Please, Shane. I need to hear what he has to say."

"If you don't mind, Lydia, I'd rather not say this in front of you."

"Gabriel, you're scaring me." Lydia stood, holding Wyatt against her. "Do we need to hide?"

His expression was guarded. "No."

Shane intervened. "Just tell us, Gabe. What happened?"

Gabriel looked from Shane to Lydia and back again. "Joseph ambushed us on the trail."

Lydia gasped. "Was anyone hurt?"

"Only one person."

"Ben or Isaac? Duncan?"

"No–o–o." He stopped. "Shane, I'd really rather discuss this in private."

"I'm not leaving," Lydia snapped. "Tell us what happened, Gabe. Please."

"If you're sure."

Lydia nodded.

"Duncan wasn't kidding when he said he had things under control." Gabe glanced over at Natalie and Nathan who had just exited the barn.

Lydia waved them over. Tildy came to the kitchen door and called the little girls in.

"Joseph came up behind us, riding fast. Duncan whipped around with his rifle raised and told him to stop."

"He didn't stop."

"No."

"Did Duncan shoot him?"

"That's where things got strange. Before Duncan could fire off a shot, Joseph ran headlong into a tree and fell from his horse."

"How bad is he?" Lydia wished she could work up some sympathy, but she couldn't. The man was nothing but evil.

"Duncan went back to check on him. Joseph hit the tree hard. We all saw it. He wasn't breathing. Joseph is—well, he's dead, Lydia."

Lydia was stunned.

Natalie buried her face in Nathan's shoulder. Nathan led her over to Lydia and Wyatt. "He can't hurt us anymore."

"No," Lydia whispered. "Just like that."

Gabriel frowned.

"I know we sound callous, Gabe, but you saw Joseph. He was horrible to us. I don't know what he was like when our mother first met him, but from my earliest memory, he was horrible to her and horrible to us."

"We saw." Shane laid a supportive hand on Lydia's arm.

"I'm sad for the person he could have been, but he never was that person."

Gabriel nodded. "Duncan sent me ahead. Ben is waiting with the others. Isaac and Duncan stayed back with Joseph. Duncan wants me to return and tell him your preferences."

Lydia shivered. "I don't want him anywhere near us, even in death."

"I'll go." Nathan started back to get his horse. "Someone will need to tend to the livestock."

"Nathan, wait." Lydia allowed Shane to take Wyatt. "I don't want you over there alone."

"I'll be fine." He smiled. "I'll check in first thing tomorrow."

"Ben told me he'd like to go back and care for the livestock," Gabriel inserted. "The workers want to go with him."

"Oh." Nathan seemed undecided.

"I need you here, Nathan. Ben needs to do this. Let him go. It'll give him something to do while he waits for Sadie."

Nathan nodded. "Gabriel? Tell him to make himself at home inside the plantation house. Tell him I'll be over in the morning to help. As for Joseph, tell Duncan we don't have a preference other than he take the body well away from here."

"Will do." Gabriel headed out.

Lydia shivered again. The words were eerily similar to the ones Joseph had said a few nights earlier about her.

"You two go on in. We'll join you in a few minutes." Shane took Lydia by the arm and held her back.

Nathan led Natalie toward the kitchen.

Shane led Lydia around to sit on the front porch swing where they'd talked their first night at the house. "I'm sorry about Joseph."

He sat down beside her and settled Wyatt in her arms. She nestled her face in Wyatt's soft curls.

"I'm not sure how to feel. I mostly feel relieved."

"I don't blame you." He put his arm around her, and she rested her head on his shoulder. "I'm sure you'll all go through some mixed emotions while you're sorting everything out."

"Nathan won't be back after tomorrow. He'll stay on to run the plantation."

"Is that a bad thing?"

"No. He loves it there and does a good job. He's a hard worker. He'll make a good plantation owner."

"What about Natalie?"

"I think she'll stay around for a while. I'm not sure she'll want to return to the place that holds so many bad memories, at least for a while." She shuddered. "At least that's how I feel."

"You know you have a place here."

She nodded against his sleeve. "She and Nathan are close. She'll return at some point, but she'll want to be here with me, too. She'll bounce back and forth until she finds her place."

"She's welcome here, too. All of you are."

"I know, and I thank you for that."

"Lydie?" Shane stopped the swing.

Lydia raised her head to look at him.

"Like I said, I know it'll take a while for you to sort everything out."

"Right. I understand."

"I just want you to know that I'm here for you while you're sorting."

She laughed. "I know that, too. And I appreciate it."

He sighed. "What I'm trying to say is, take your time grieving, adjusting, and making whatever decisions that need to be made. I'm going to be right here, waiting until things settle. After that, I'd like you to consider a future with me."

She nestled back in his arms. "I think I'm going to enjoy the settling process."

He kissed the top of her head and pulled her close. "Me, too, Lydie. Me, too."

A Letter To Our Readers

Dear Reader:
In order that we might better contribute to your reading enjoyment, we would appreciate your taking a few minutes to respond to the following questions. We welcome your comments and read each form and letter we receive. When completed, please return to the following:

Fiction Editor
Heartsong Presents
PO Box 719
Uhrichsville, Ohio 44683

1. Did you enjoy reading *The Displaced Belle* by Paige Winship Dooly?
   ❑ Very much! I would like to see more books by this author!
   ❑ Moderately. I would have enjoyed it more if

   ____

   ____

   ____

2. Are you a member of **Heartsong Presents**? ❑ Yes ❑ No
   If no, where did you purchase this book? ________________

   ____

3. How would you rate, on a scale from 1 (poor) to 5 (superior), the cover design? ____________________________

4. On a scale from 1 (poor) to 10 (superior), please rate the following elements.

____	Heroine	____	Plot
____	Hero	____	Inspirational theme
____	Setting	____	Secondary characters

5. These characters were special because? ____________________

____

____

6. How has this book inspired your life? ____________________

____

____

7. What settings would you like to see covered in future **Heartsong Presents** books? ____________________

____

____

8. What are some inspirational themes you would like to see treated in future books? ____________________

____

____

9. Would you be interested in reading other **Heartsong Presents** titles? ❑ Yes ❑ No

10. Please check your age range:

❑ Under 18 ❑ 18-24
❑ 25-34 ❑ 35-45
❑ 46-55 ❑ Over 55

Name ____________________________________

Occupation ____________________________________

Address ____________________________________

City, State, Zip ____________________________________

E-mail ____________________________________